Donna Kooler's 555 Country Cross-Stitch Patterns

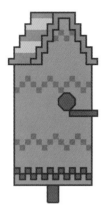

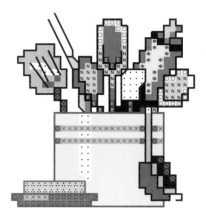

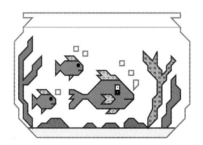

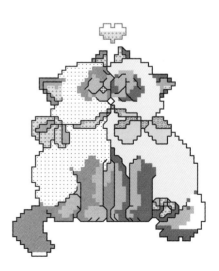

Donna Kooler's 555 Country Cross-Stitch Patterns

Sterling Publishing Co., Inc. New York

Kooler Design Studio, Inc.

Editor: Priscilla Timm
President: Donna Kooler
Executive Vice President: Linda Gillum
Vice President: Priscilla Timm
Creative Director: Deanna West
Executive Assistant: Loretta Heden
Design Staff: Linda Gillum, Nancy Rossi,
Barbara Baatz, Jorja Hernandez, and Sandy Orton
Contributing Artists: Donna Yuen and Pam Johnson
Staff: Sara Angle, Anita Forfang, Virginia Hanley-Rivett,
Marsha Hinkson, Arlis Johnson, Lori Patton,
Char Randolph, and Giana Shaw

Chapelle Ltd.

Owner: Jo Packham
Editor: Karmen Quinney
Staff: Marie Barber, Ann Bear, Areta Bingham,
Kass Burchett, Rebecca Christensen, Marilyn Goff,
Amber Hansen, Shirley Heslop, Holly Hollingsworth,
Shawn Hsu, Susan Jorgensen, Pauline Locke,
Ginger Mikkelsen, Barbara Milburn, Linda Orton,
Rhonda Rainey, Leslie Ridenour, and Cindy Stoeckl
Photographer: Kevin Dilley Hazen Photography Studio
Photography Stylist: Leslie Liechty

Dedication

Our, studio was filled with an extra bit of laughter, chatter, and friendship while working upon this challenging project. It might be equated to a bee. Everyone was eagerly contributing something of value, their artistic talents, wonderful creative ideas, and beautiful stitching. The results of all this talent is a wonderful patchwork collection of over 500 cross-stitch designs bound together for your creative enjoyment.

We wanted the chapters to express our feeling for home and family as well as the giving and sharing that cross-stitchers always exhibit. So, we would like to dedicate this book to all who share this love and pass along personal expressions of beauty while creating future heirlooms for generations to come.

Library of Congress Cataloging-in-Publication Data Available

10 9 8 7 6 5 4 3 2 1

A Sterling/Chapelle Book
First paperback edition published in 2000 by
Sterling Publishing Company, Inc.
387 Park Avenue South, New York, N.Y. 10016
Produced by Chapelle Ltd.
P.O. Box 9252, Newgate Station, Ogden, Utah 84409
© 1998 by Chapelle Ltd.
Distributed in Canada by Sterling Publishing
℅ Canadian Manda Group, One Atlantic Avenue, Suite 105
Toronto, Ontario, Canada M6K 3E7
Distributed in Great Britain and Europe by Cassell PLC,
Wellington House, 125 Strand, London WC2R 0BB, England
Distributed in Australia by Capricorn Link (Australia) Pty Ltd.
P.O. Box 6651, Baulkham Hills, Business Centre, NSW 2153, Australia
Printed in China
All rights reserved

Sterling ISBN 0-8069-0330-9 Trade
         0-8069-7779-5 Paper

If you have any questions or comments or would like information on specialty products featured in this book, please contact: Chapelle Ltd., Inc., P.O. Box 9252 Ogden, UT 84409 (801) 621-2777 • FAX (801) 621-2788

Every effort has been made to ensure that all the information in this book is accurate. However, due to differing conditions, tools, and individual skills, the publisher cannot be responsible for any injuries, losses, and other damages which may result from the use of the information in this book.

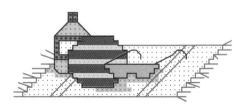

Contents

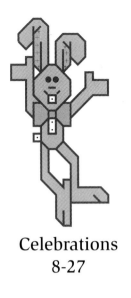

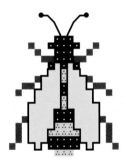

General Instructions

Introduction

Contained in this book are over 555 counted cross-stitch designs.

For each of the six chapters herein, samplers have been stitched and photographed. The samplers have been graphed and fall on the pages following the photograph.

The remaining designs in each chapter are not stitched nor photographed. Each page of graphed designs has its own color code.

To create one-of-a-kind motifs, vary colors in the graphed designs. The stitching possibilities will prove endless.

Fabric for Cross-stitch

Counted cross-stitch is usually worked on even-weave fabrics. These fabrics are manufactured specifically for counted-thread embroidery and are woven with the same number of vertical as horizontal threads per inch.

Because the number of threads in the fabric is equal in each direction, each stitch will be the same size. The number of threads per inch in even-weave fabrics determines the size of a finished design.

Number of Strands

The number of strands used per stitch varies depending on the fabric used. Generally, the rule to follow for cross-stitching is three strands on Aida 11, two strands on Aida 14, one or two strands on Aida 18 (depending on desired thickness of stitches) and one strand on Hardanger 22.

For back-stitching, use one strand on all fabrics. When completing a french knot, use two strands and one wrap on all fabrics.

Preparing Fabric

Cut fabric at least 3" larger on all sides than finished design size to ensure enough space for desired assembly. If the design is used to embellish a project that will be finished further, check instructions for specific fabric allowances. A 3" margin is the minimum amount of space that allows for comfortably finishing the edges of the design.

To prevent fraying, whipstitch or machine-zigzag along raw edges or apply liquid fray preventer.

Needles for Cross-stitch

Needles should slip easily through fabric holes without piercing fabric threads. For fabric with 11 or fewer threads per inch, use a tapestry needle size 24; for 14 threads per inch, use a tapestry needle size 24 or 26; for 18 or more threads per inch, use a tapestry needle size 26. Never leave needle in design area of fabric. It may leave rust or a permanent impression on fabric.

Finished Design Size

To determine size of finished design, divide stitch count by number of threads per inch of fabric. When design is stitched over two threads, divide stitch count by half the threads per inch.

Floss

For each sampler and each page of graphed designs there is a color code. All numbers and color names on this code represent DMC brands of floss. Use 18" lengths of floss. For best coverage, separate strands. Dampen with wet sponge. Then put together number of strands required for fabric used.

Centering the Design

Fold the fabric in half horizontally, then vertically. Place a pin in the fold point to mark the center. Locate the center of the design on the graph. To help in centering the samplers, arrows are provided at left center and top center. Begin stitching all designs at the center point of graph and fabric.

Securing the Floss

Insert needle up from the underside of the fabric at starting point. Hold 1" of thread behind the fabric and stitch over it, securing with the first few stitches. To finish thread, run under four or more stitches on the back of the design. Never knot floss, unless working on clothing.

Another method of securing floss is the waste knot. Knot floss and insert needle from the right side of the fabric about 1" from design area. Work several stitches over the thread to secure. Cut off the knot later.

Carrying Floss

To carry floss, weave floss under the previously worked stitches on the back. Do not carry thread across any fabric that is not or will not be stitched. Loose threads, especially dark ones, will show through the fabric.

Cleaning Completed Work

When stitching is complete, soak fabric in cold water with a mild soap for five to 10 minutes. Rinse well and roll in a towel to remove excess water. Do not wring. Place work face down on a dry towel and iron on warm setting until the fabric is dry.

Cross-stitch (X st)

Stitches are done in a row or, if necessary, one at a time in an area. Stitching is done by coming up through a hole between woven threads at A. Then, go down at B, the hole diagonally across from A. Come back up at C and down at D, etc. Complete the top stitches to create an "X". All top stitches should lie in the same direction. Come up at E and go down at B, come up at C and go down at F, etc.

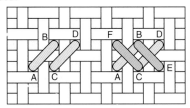

Backstitch (BS)

Pull the needle through at the point marked A. Then go down one opening to the right, at B. Then, come back up at C. Now, go down one opening to the right, this time at "A".

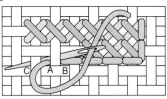

French Knot (FK)

Bring needle up at A, using two strands of embroidery floss. Loosely wrap floss once around needle. Place needle at B, next to A. Pull floss taut as needle is pushed down through fabric. Carry floss across back of work between knots.

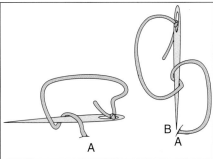

Long Stitch (LS)

Bring needle up at A; go down at B. Pull flat. Repeat A–B for each stitch. The length of the stitch should be the same as the length of the line on the design chart.

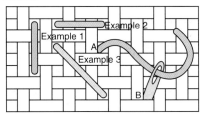

Lazy Daisy (LD)

Bring the needle up at A. Keep the thread flat, untwisted, and full. Put the needle down through fabric at B and up through at C, keeping the thread under the needle to form a loop. Pull the thread through, leaving the loop loose and full. To hold the loop in place, go down on other side of thread near C, forming a straight stitch over loop.

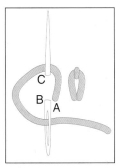

Bead Attachment (Bds)

Beads should sit facing the same direction as the top cross-stitch. Make first half of stitch in opposite direction from remainder of the piece. Come up as if to cross and pick up bead before going down in opposite corner. To strengthen stitch, come up again in lower corner and either go through bead again or split threads to lay around bead and go down in opposite corner.

Celebrations

Bottom Left

Bottom Middle

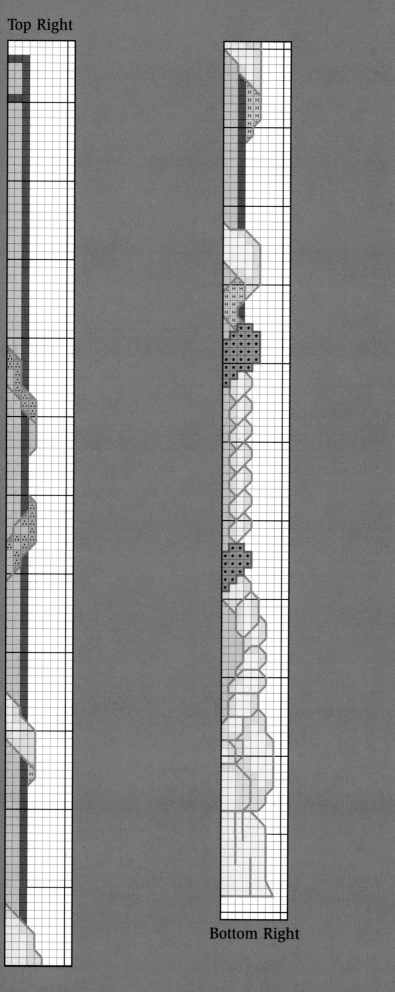

Top Right

Bottom Right

DMC Floss

	X st	BS	FK	LS
White	⊡			
3823	☐			
3078	◱			
745	△			
744	▨			
743	H			
742	✳			
725	⊡			
783		⌐		╱
951	▨			
945	−			
3824	▨			
352	○			
350	▨	⌐	●	
818	▨			
963	+			
3326	▨			╱
961	▨	⌐	●	
223	▨			
3722	▨	⌐		
3609	★			╱
211	▨			
210	▨			
341	W			
747	☐			
3761	K			
807		⌐		
3756	⊠			
800	▨			
799	▨			
798	▨	⌐	●	
955	▨			
954	▨			
562		⌐		
989	▨			
988		⌐		
437	N			
3776	▨			
758	▨			
356	▨			
632	■	⌐		
762	▨			
318	▨			
317		⌐	●	
310	▨	⌐	●	

DMC Floss

	X st	BS	FK
White	·		
745			
743	−		
742			
605	⊡		
3326	+		
3609			
3607		⌐	
209		⌐	
552		⌐	
747			
792		⌐	●
955			
954	◎		
912			
435			
415			
413		⌐	●

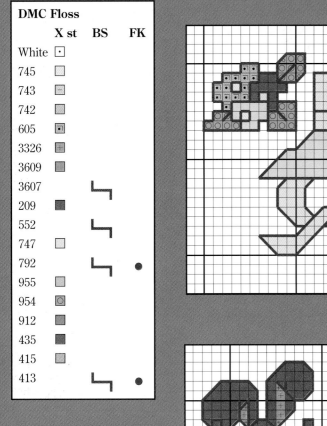

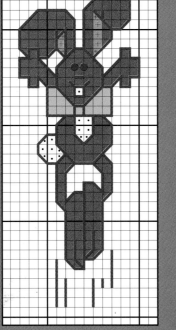

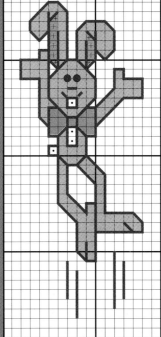

16

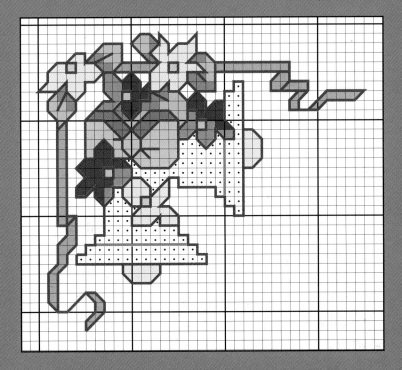

DMC Floss

	X st	BS	FK
White	·		
745			
742			
818			
605	⊙		
3326	+		
602		⌐	
335		⌐	●
3609			
3607		⌐	
554			
552		⌐	
209			
208		⌐	
800			
334			
792		⌐	●
955			
912			
762	△		
415			
317		⌐	
413		⌐	●

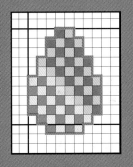

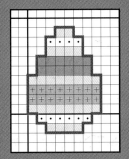

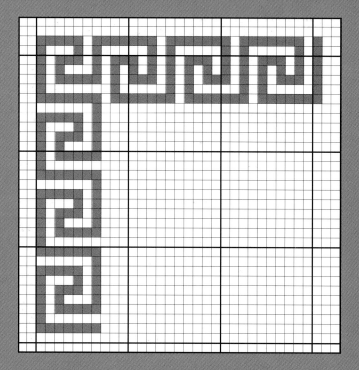

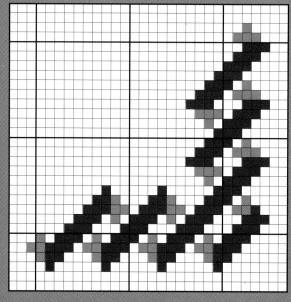

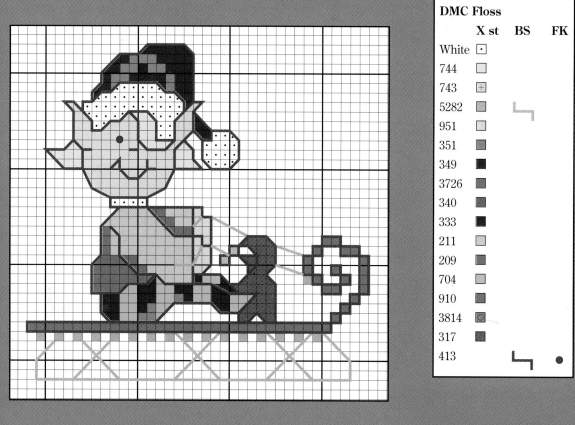

DMC Floss

	X st	BS	FK
White	⊡		
744	▦		
743	⊞		
5282	▦	⌐	
951	▦		
351	▦		
349	■		
3726	▦		
340	▦		
333	■		
211	▦		
209	▦		
704	▦		
910	▦		
3814	▣		
317	▦		
413		⌐	●

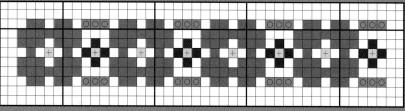

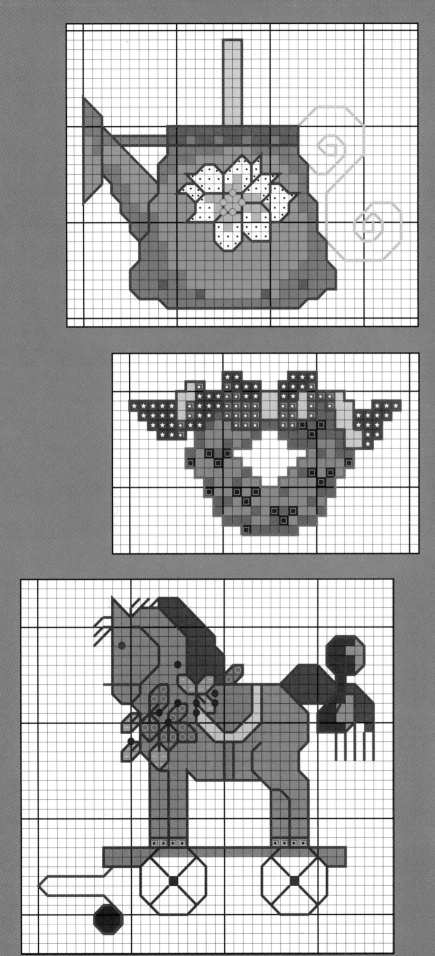

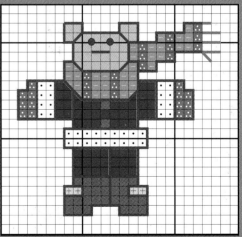

DMC Floss

	X st	BS	FK
White	·		
725	+		
676			
729	⊡		
5282		⌐	●
351			
349	■		
817		⌐	●
816	⊡		
3688			
3687			
800			
799			
798	⊡		
796	★	⌐	
913			
911	◉		
910	⊡	⌐	
992			
3814			
702			
700		⌐	
3779			
3776			
400	■		
300		⌐	
317	■		
413		⌐	●

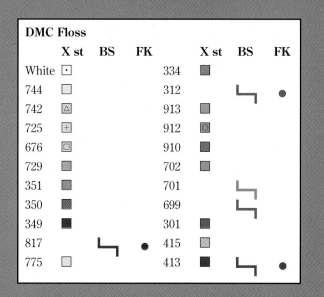

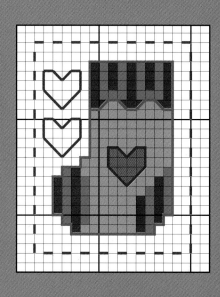

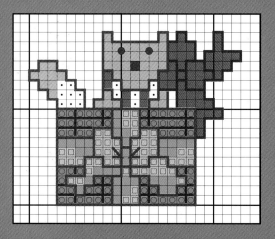

20

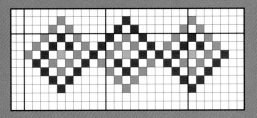

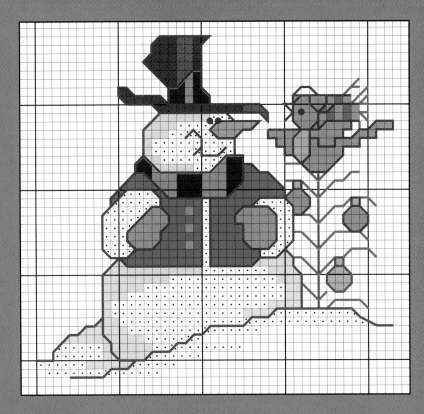

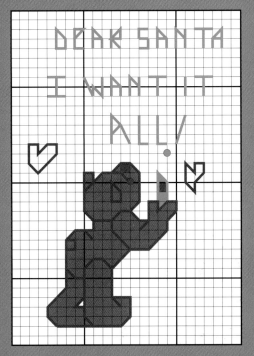

DEAR SANTA I WANT IT ALL!

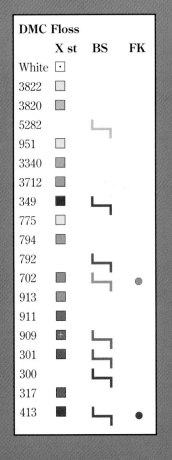

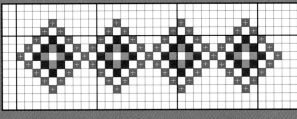

DMC Floss

	X st	BS	FK
White	·		
3822	▨		
3820	▨		
5282		⌐	
951	▨		
3340	▨		
3712	▨		
349	▨	⌐	
775	▨		
794	▨		
792	▨	⌐	
702	▨	⌐	●
913	▨		
911	▨		
909	+	⌐	
301	▨	⌐	
300	▨	⌐	
317	▨		
413	▨	⌐	●

DMC Floss

	X st	BS		X st	BS	FK
White	·		954			
3823			913			
3822			911			
5282		⌐	909		⌐	
951			3776			
351			301			
349			400		⌐	
962			317			
775			413		⌐	●
322		⌐				

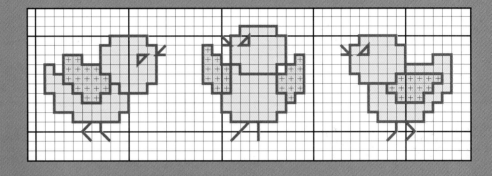

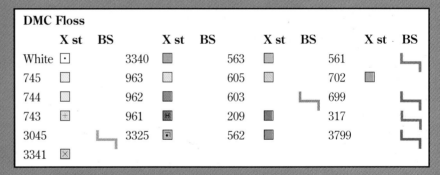

DMC Floss

	X st	BS		X st	BS		X st	BS		X st	BS
White	·		3340	▨		563	▨		561		⌐
745	▢		963	▨		605	▨		702	▨	⌐
744	▢		962	▨		603		⌐	699		⌐
743	⊞		961	⊞		209	▨		317		⌐
3045		⌐	3325	⊡		562	▨		3799		⌐
3341	⊠										

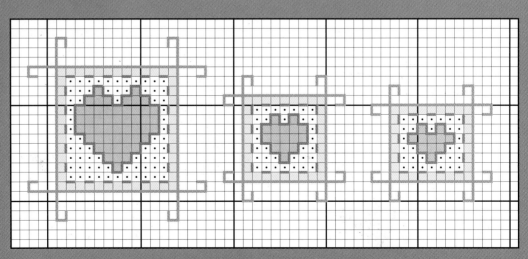

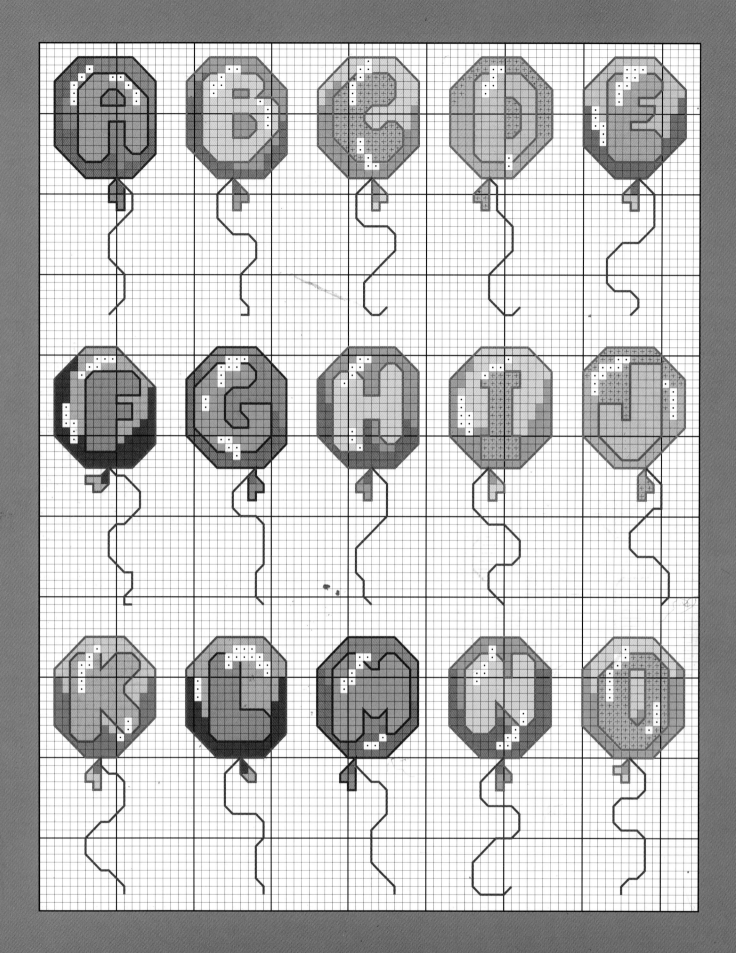

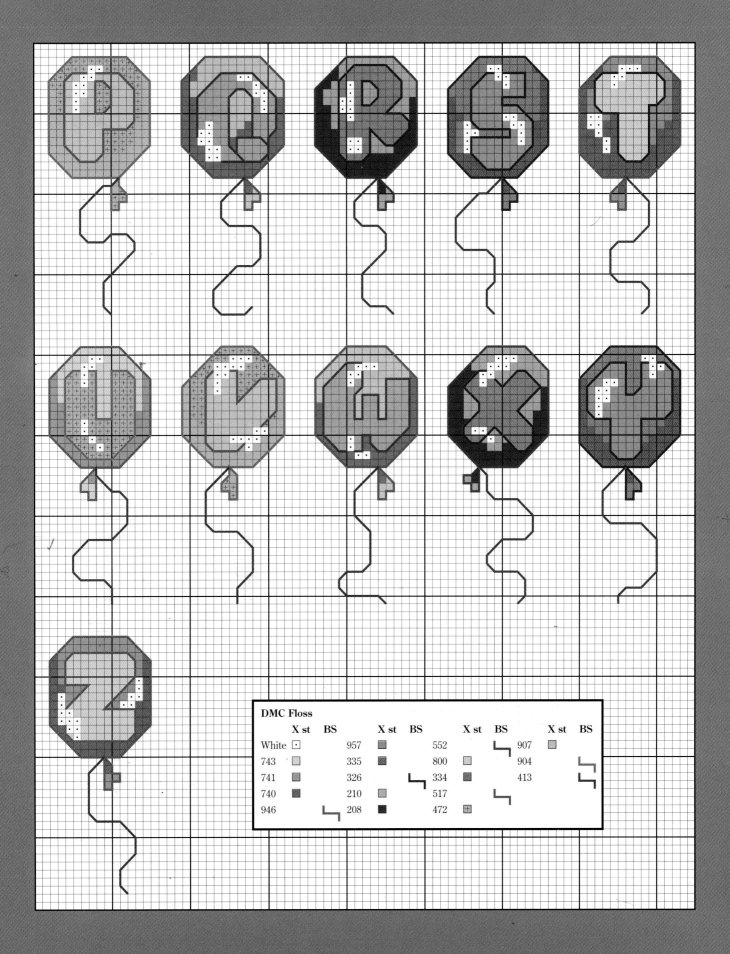

DMC Floss

	X st	BS		X st	BS		X st	BS		X st	BS
White	·		957			552			907		
743			335			800			904		
741			326			334			413		
740			210			517					
946		⌐	208			472					

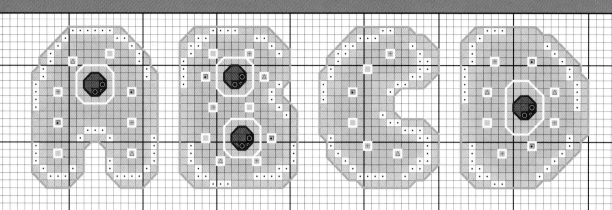

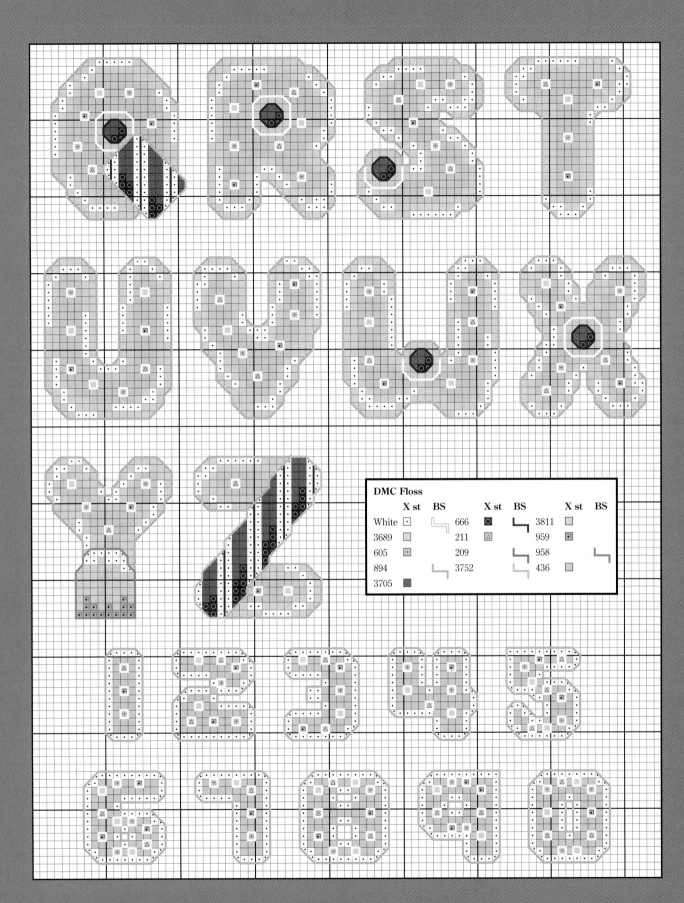

DMC Floss

	X st	BS	X st	BS	X st	BS
White	·	⌐ 666	●	⌐ 3811	▨	
3689	▨	211	▲	3959	▨	
605	⊞	209		958	⌐	
894		⌐ 3752		436	▨	⌐
3705	▨					

Favorite Things

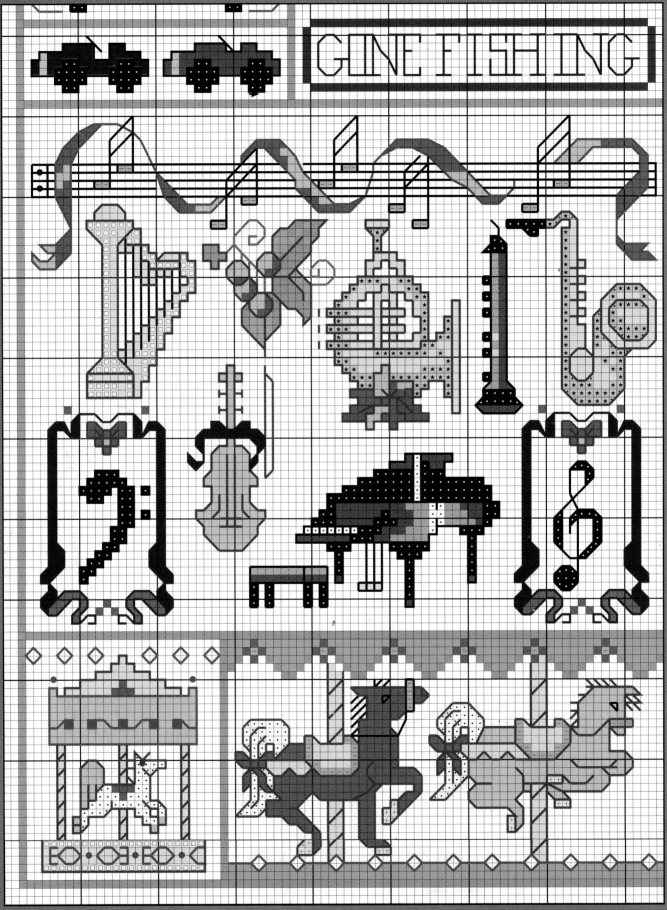

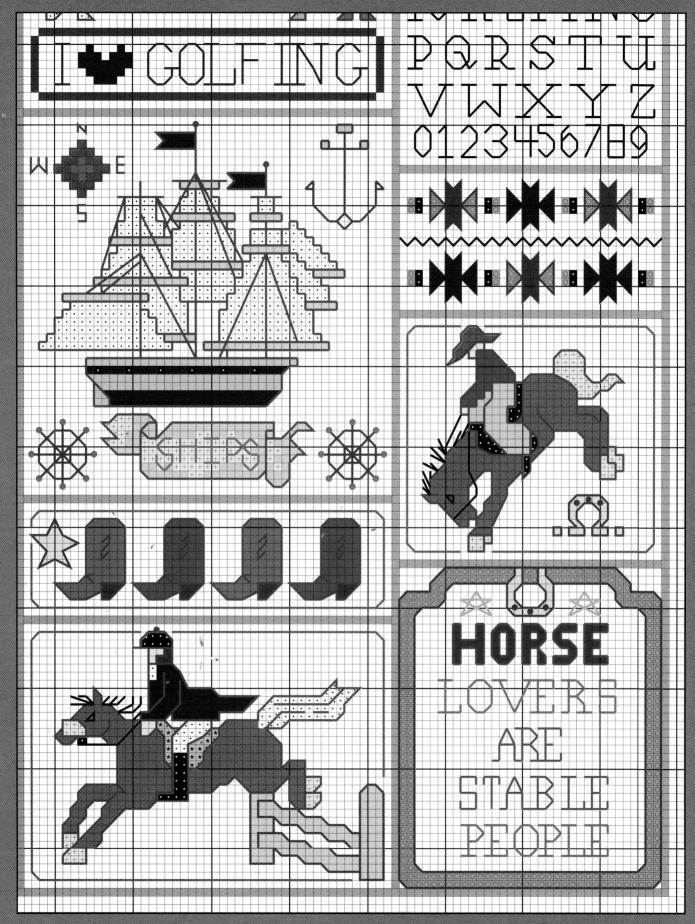

I ♥ GOLFING

PQRSTU
VWXYZ
0123456789

SHIPS

HORSE
LOVERS
ARE
STABLE
PEOPLE

Code for Pages 30-33

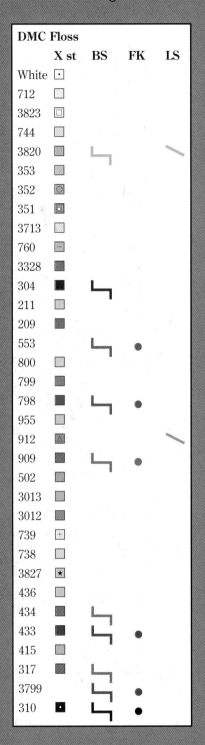

DMC Floss

	X st	BS	FK	LS
White	·			
712				
3823				
744				
3820		⌐		/
353				
352	⊙			
351				
3713				
760	–			
3328				
304	■	⌐		
211				
209				
553		⌐	●	
800				
799				
798	■	⌐	●	
955				
912	△			/
909		⌐	●	
502				
3013				
3012				
739	+			
738				
3827	★			
436				
434		⌐		
433		⌐	●	
415				
317		⌐		
3799		⌐	●	
310	■	⌐	●	

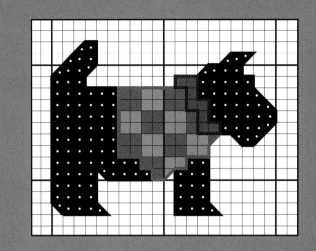

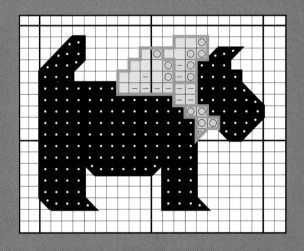

Code for Pages 34-35

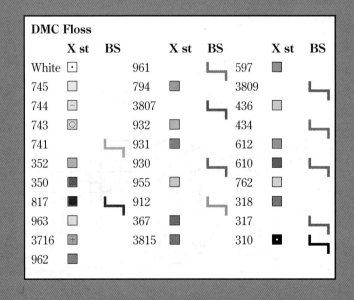

DMC Floss

	X st	BS		X st	BS		X st	BS
White	·		961		⌐	597		
745			794			3809		⌐
744	–		3807		⌐	436		
743	⊙		932			434		⌐
741		⌐	931			612		
352			930			610		⌐
350			955			762		
817		⌐	912		⌐	318		⌐
963			367			317		⌐
3716	+		3815			310	■	⌐
962								

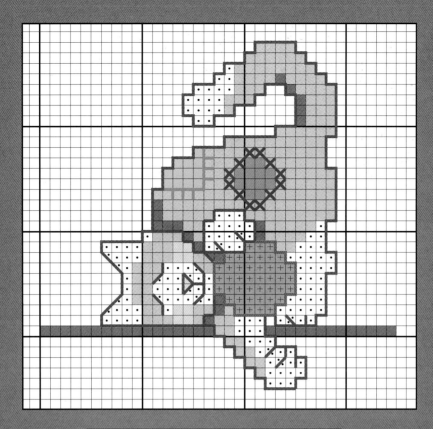

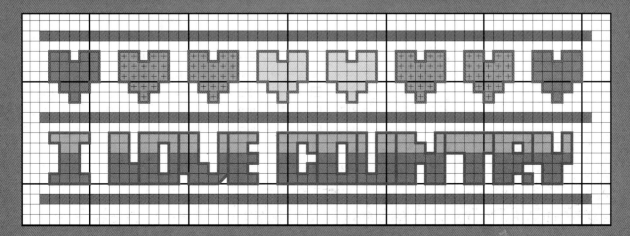

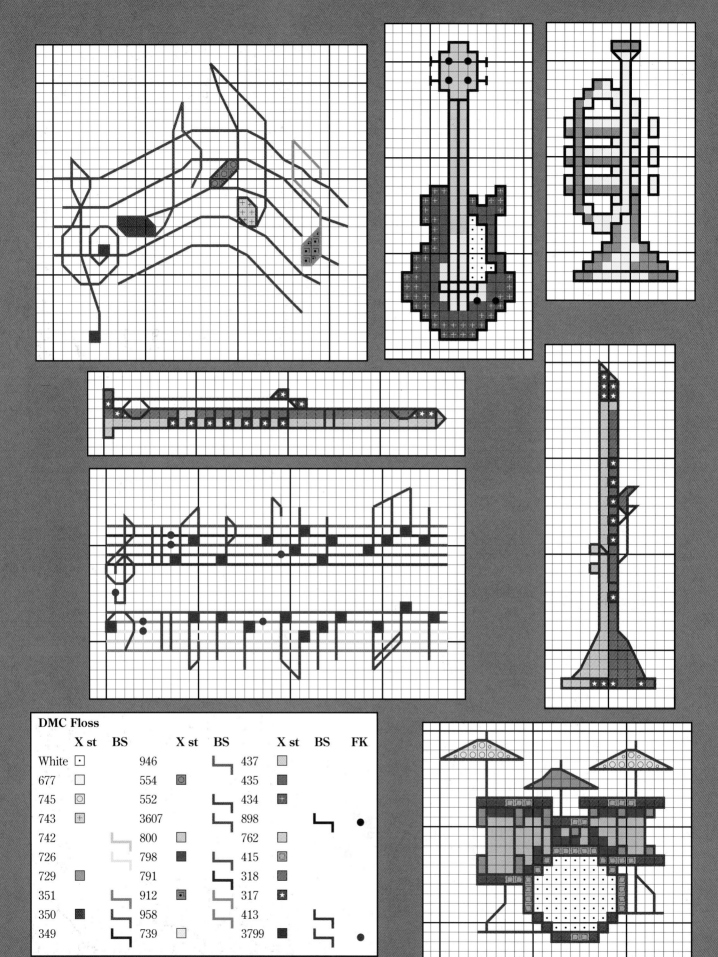

DMC Floss

	X st	BS		X st	BS		X st	BS	FK
White	·		946			437			
677			554	◎		435			
745	◎		552			434	+		
743	+		3607			898			•
742			800			762			
726			798			415	▣		
729			791			318			
351			912	⊡		317	★		
350			958			413			
349			739			3799			•

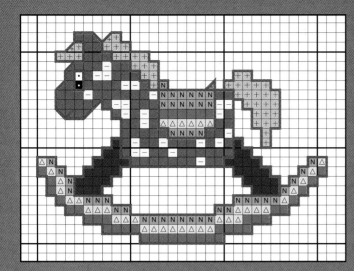

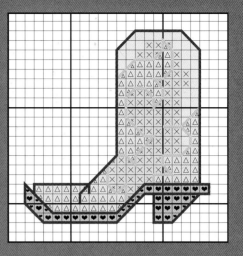

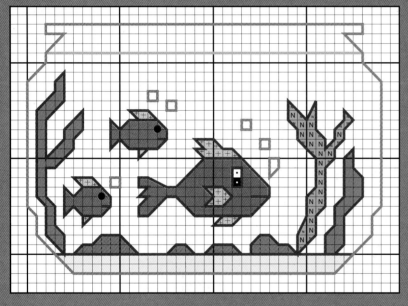

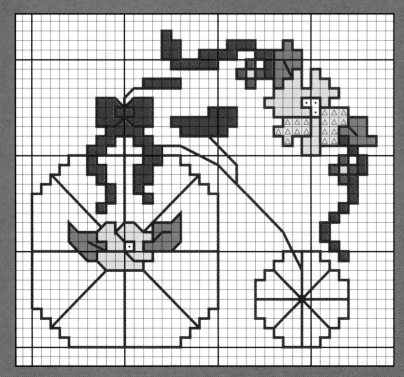

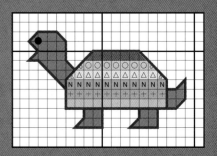

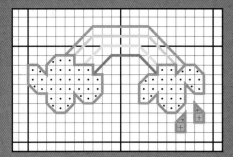

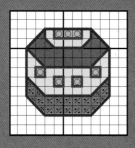

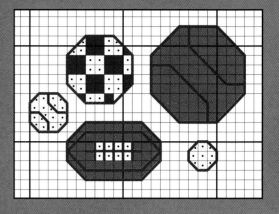

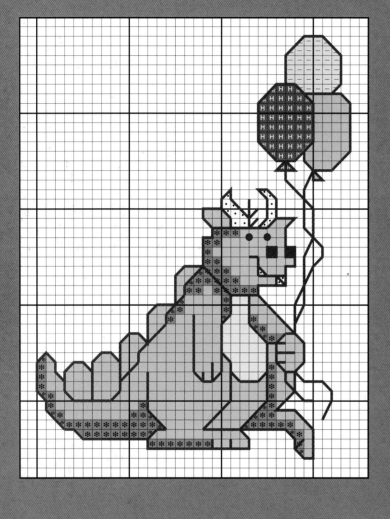

DMC Floss			
	X st	BS	FK
White	⊡		
745	▢		
744	⊟		⌐
3827	⊞		⌐
946	H		
3341		⌐	
899		⌐	
353	⊙		
350	◼	⌐	
666		L	
209	◼	⌐	
208		L	
800	⊠		
3755	▢		
3325	⊞		
826	◼	⌐	
799	▨		
798		⌐	
796		L	
987		⌐	
955	▢		
912	✳		
921	◼		
415	▢		
3799	◼	L	●

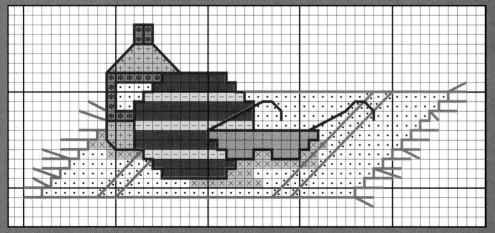

DMC Floss

	X st	BS		X st	BS		X st	BS		X st	BS		X st	BS	FK
White	·		963	▫		211	▫		959	▬		436	♥			
Ecru	▬		776	⊠		210	△		958	▪		920				
712	▫		3326	H		209	▪		563	▫		838	▪			
745	◎		353	◎		208	■		702	▫		318	▪			
743	✳		335			775	▫		988	N		413	▪			●
742	▪		666	■		826	▪		986	▪		3799				●
740	▪		3609	▨		322	▪		437	▫						
3341	△		3607	▨		798	▪									

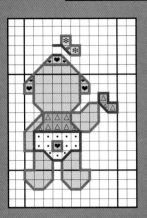

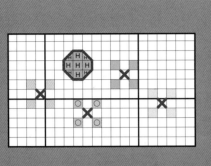

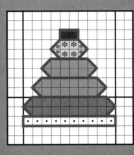

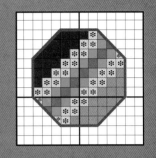

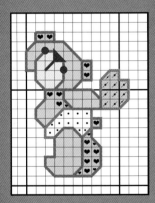

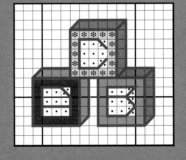

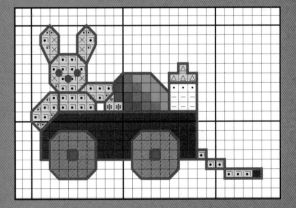

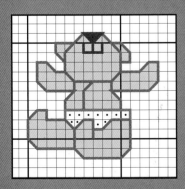

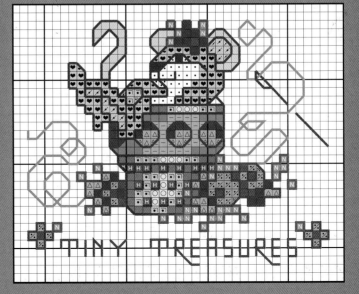

MINY TREASURES

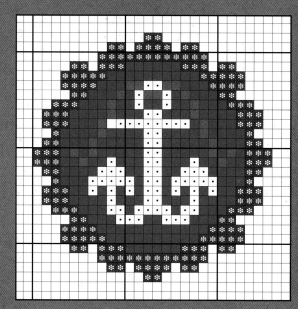

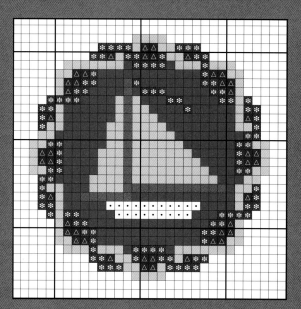

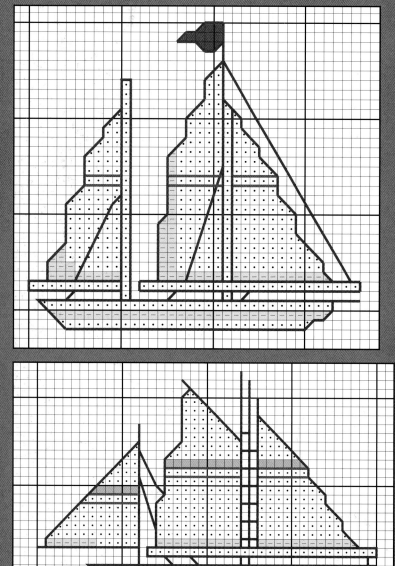

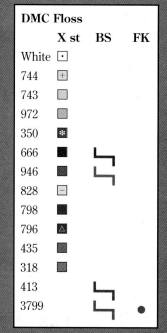

DMC Floss			
	X st	BS	FK
White	·		
744	+		
743			
972			
350	*		
666		⌐	
946		⌐	
828	–		
798			
796	△		
435			
318			
413		⌐	
3799		⌐	•

DMC Floss

	X st		X st	FK		X st		X st	BS	FK
745	☐	349	▣		826	▨	415	▨		
743	✳	666	◼	●	931	★	318	▨		
725	▨	814	◼		563		413	▨		
776	⊠	209	▨		702	▨	3799	◼		●
899	M	775	☐		437	▨	310	◼		●
351	▨	3325	+		435	▨				

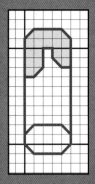

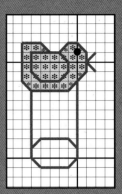

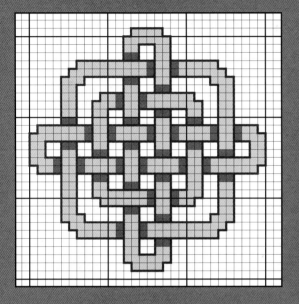

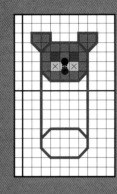

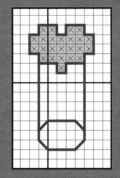

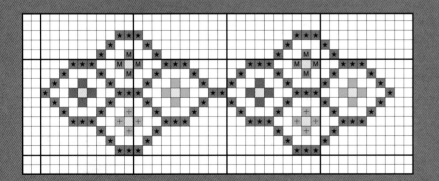

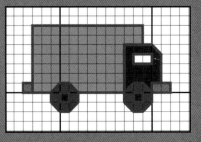

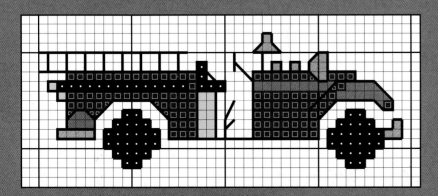

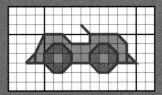

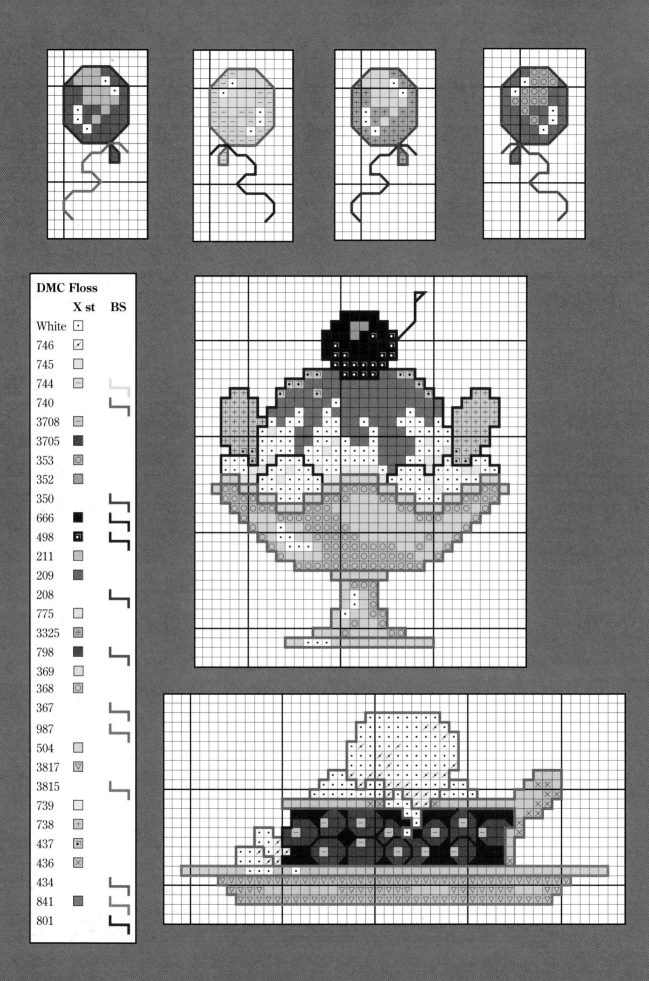

DMC Floss

	X st	BS
White	⊡	
746	⊘	
745	▨	
744	▭	⌐
740		⌐
3708	▭	
3705	▨	
353	◉	
352	▨	
350		⌐
666	■	⌐
498	◙	⌐
211	▨	
209	▨	
208		⌐
775	▨	
3325	⊞	
798	■	⌐
369	▨	
368	◎	
367		⌐
987		⌐
504	▨	
3817	▽	
3815		⌐
739	▨	
738	⊞	
437	◙	
436	✕	
434		⌐
841	▨	⌐
801		⌐

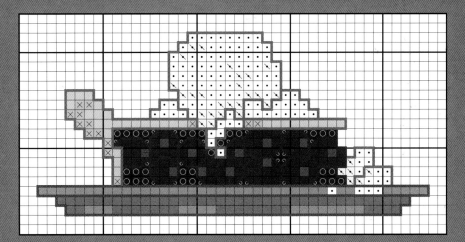

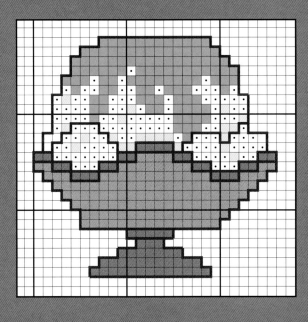

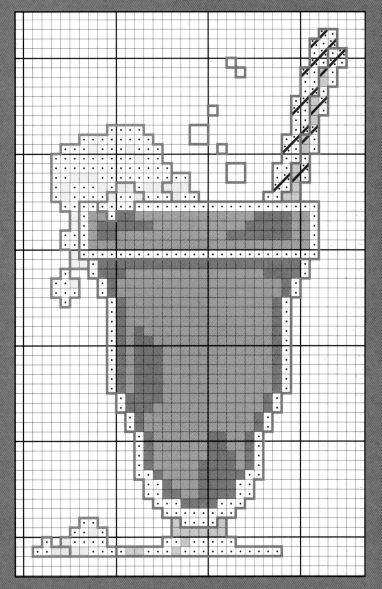

DMC Floss

	X st	BS		X st	BS
White	⊡		823	◉	
746	◪		739	▢	
352	▨		738	⊞	
666		⌐	436	⊠	
498		⌐	434		⌐
224	▨		842	▨	
223	▨		841	▨	⌐
3721		⌐	801		⌐
312	▨		762	▨	
336	▪		414		⌐
939		⌐			

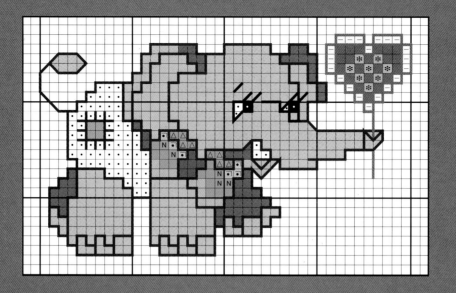

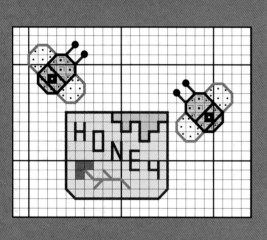

DMC Floss

	X st	BS		X st	BS		X st	BS	FK
White	·		335	▨		958	▦	⌐	
Ecru	—		326	■	⌐	563	N		⌐
745	☐		211	▨		562	▦		⌐
743	·☐		210	△		3774	☐		
3827	☐		209	▦		3779	▢		
783	▦	⌐	800	☐		3778	▦		
781	△		3325	+		632	⊡	⌐	
3341	◎		334	▦		762	☐		
605	❋		798	▦		318	▧		
603	▨	⌐	312	▦	⌐	317	❋	⌐	
776	☐		964	☐		413	■	⌐	●
3326	▨		959	—		310	⊡	⌐	●

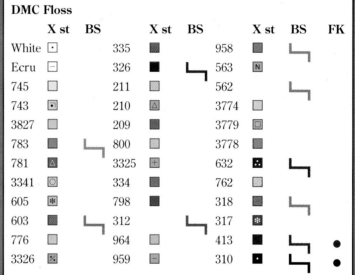

44

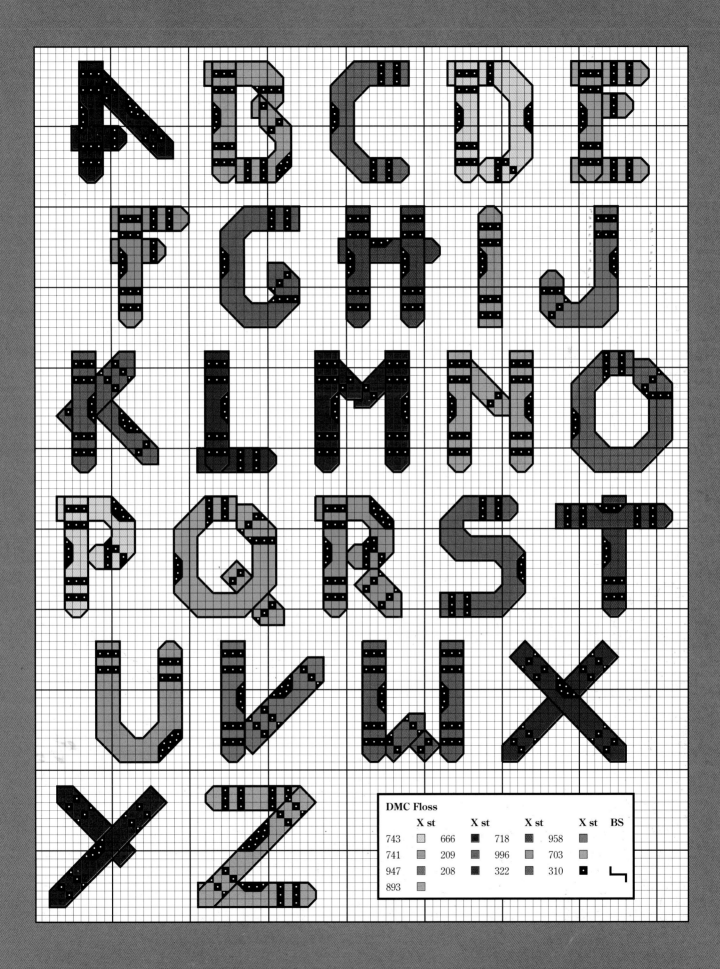

DMC Floss

	X st		X st		X st		X st		BS
743		666		718		958			
741		209		996		703			
947		208		322		310			
893									

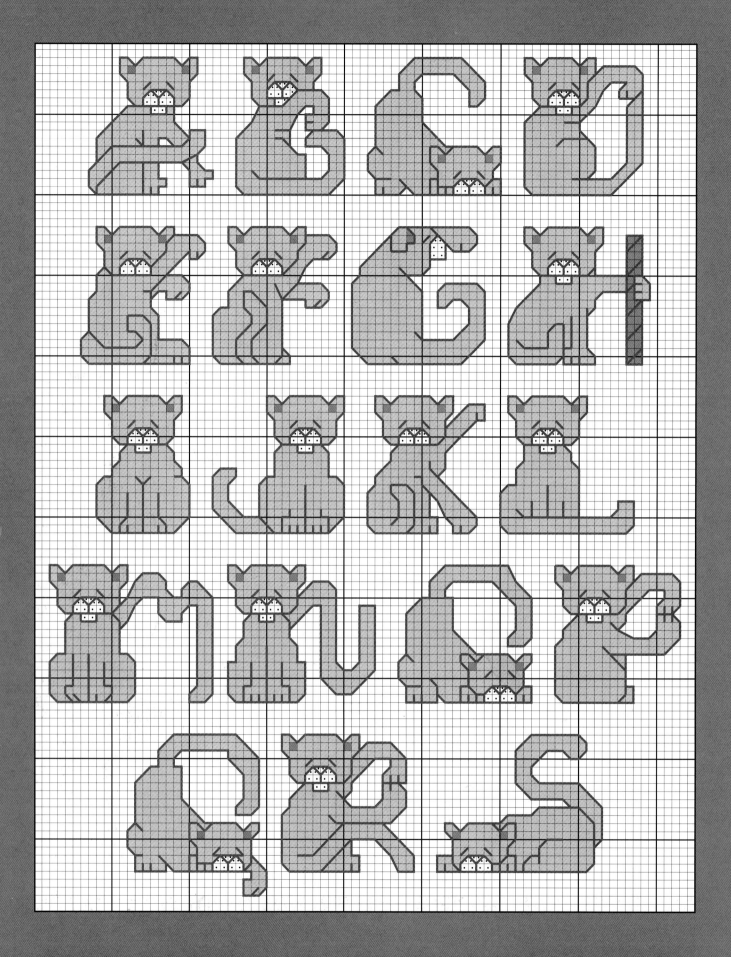

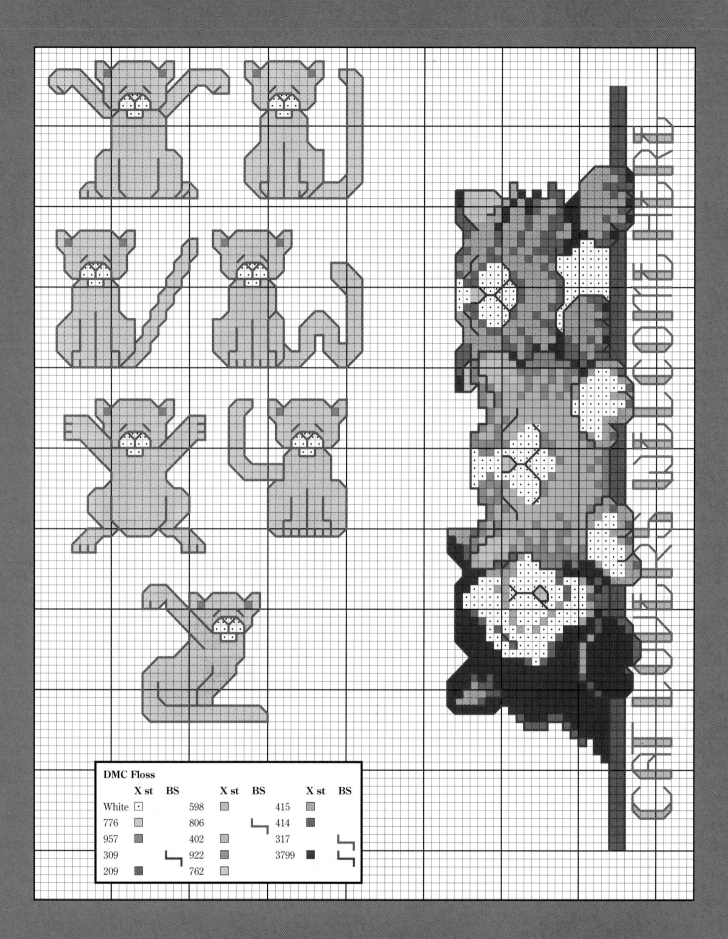

DMC Floss

	X st	BS		X st	BS		X st	BS
White	·		598			415		
776			806		414			
957			402		317			
309			922		3799			
209			762					

Home Sweet Home

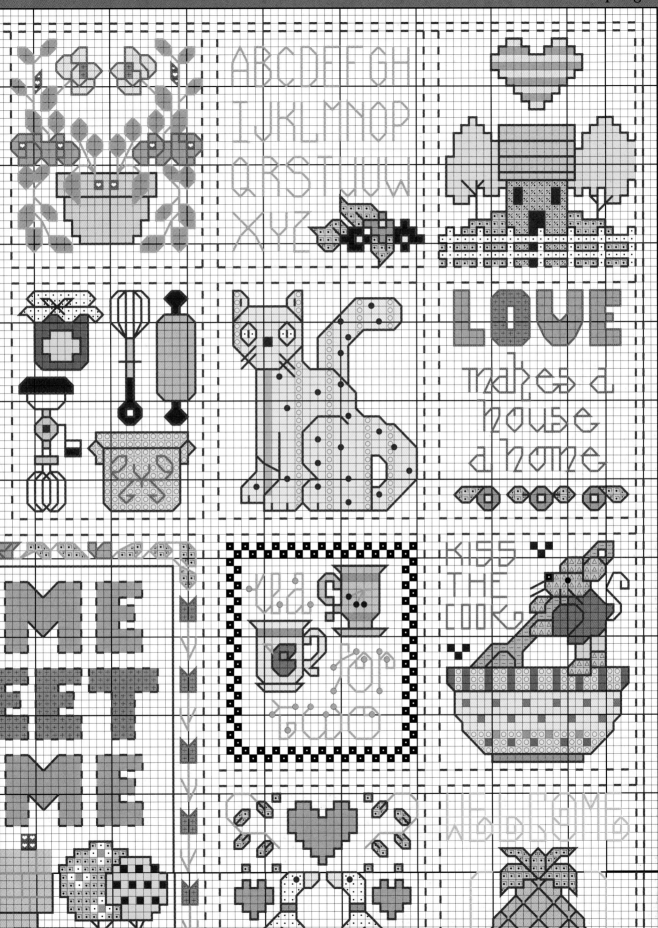

Bottom Left

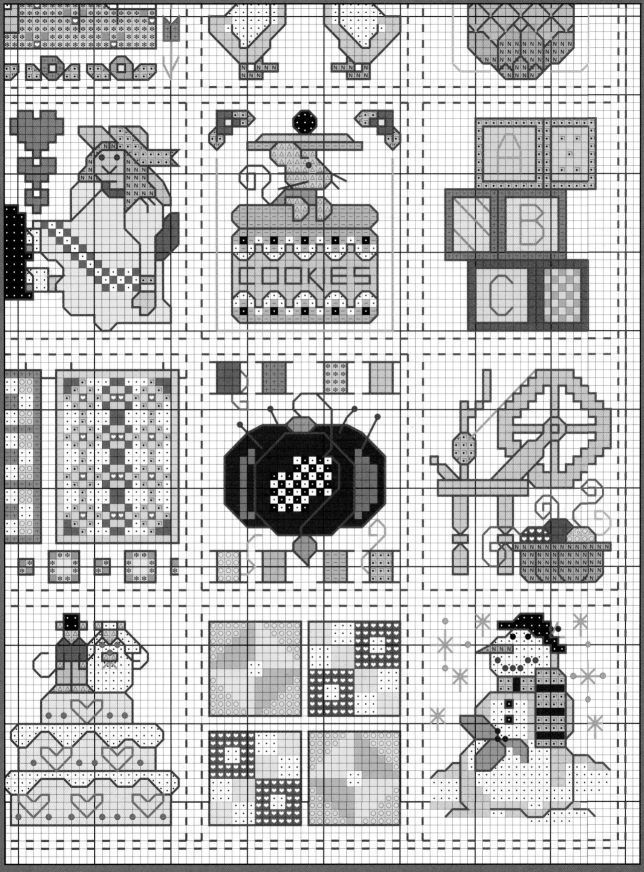

Bottom Right

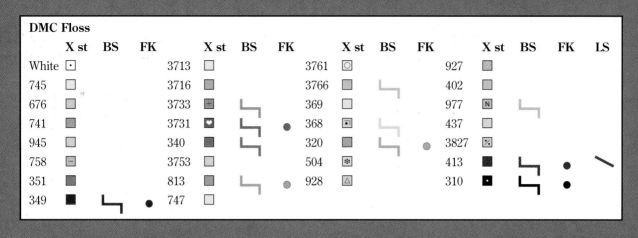

DMC Floss

	X st	BS	FK		X st	BS	FK		X st	BS	FK		X st	BS	FK	LS
White	⊡			3713	▨			3761	◉			927	▨			
745	▢			3716	▨			3766	▨		⌐	402	▨			
676	▨			3733	⊞	⌐		369	▢		⌐	977	N	⌐		
741	▨			3731	♥	⌐	●	368	⊡			437	▨			
945	▨			340	▨	⌐		320	▨	⌐	●	3827	▨			
758	⊟			3753	▨			504	✳			413	■	⌐	●	
351	▨			813	▨	⌐	●	928	△			310	▣	⌐	●	╱
349	■	⌐	●	747	▢											

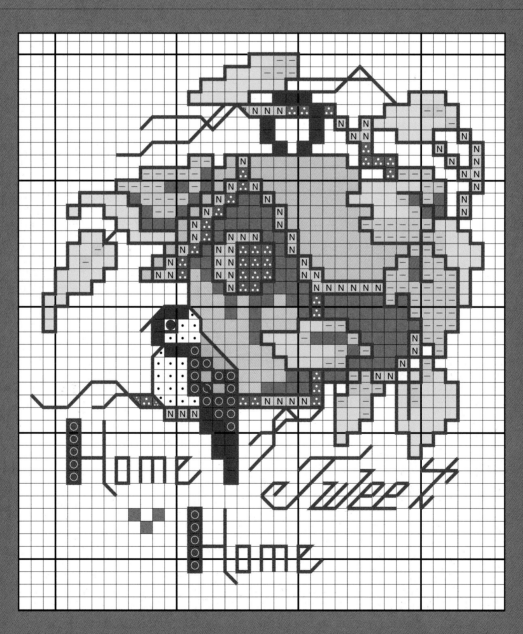

DMC Floss

	X st	BS		X st	BS	FK
White	·		472	▨		
676	▨		907	+		
351	▨		989	▨		
350	▨		986	■	⌐	
349	■		739	▨		
817		⌐	738	▨		
899	▨		437	N		
321	▣		435	▨		
211	▨		434	▨		
209	▨		433	■	⌐	
369	▨		402	▨		
368	−		301	◎		
367	▨		3799	■	⌐	●
772	⊠					

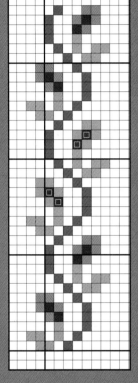

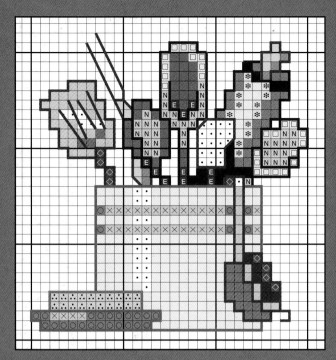

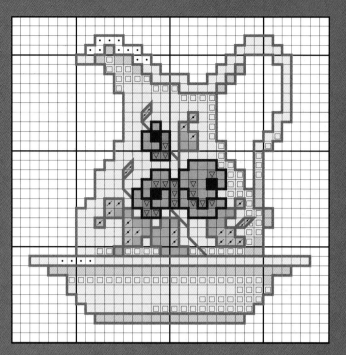

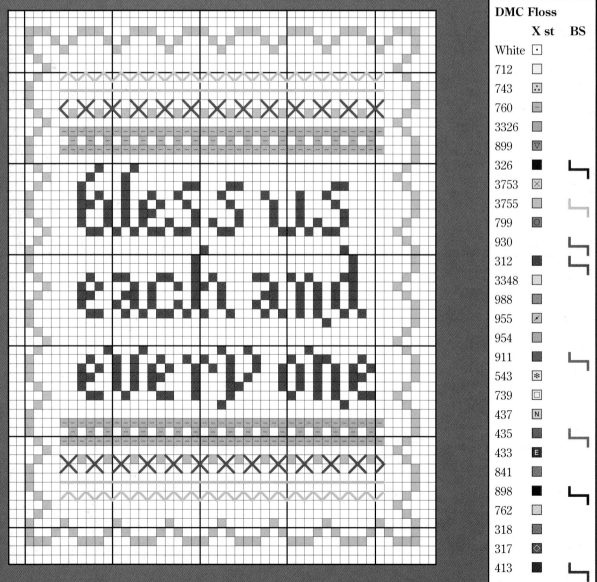

DMC Floss

	X st	BS
White	⊡	
712	☐	
743	⊡	
760	⊟	
3326	▨	
899	▽	
326	■	⌐
3753	⊠	
3755	▨	⌐
799	◎	
930	■	⌐
312	■	⌐
3348	☐	
988	▨	
955	▨	
954	▨	
911	■	⌐
543	✳	
739	☐	
437	N	
435	▨	⌐
433	E	
841	▨	
898	■	⌐
762	☐	
318	▨	
317	◈	
413	■	⌐

DMC Floss

	X st	BS		X st		X st	BS
676			813		319		
223			825		420		
3721			320		310		

Plenty and Grace be to this Place

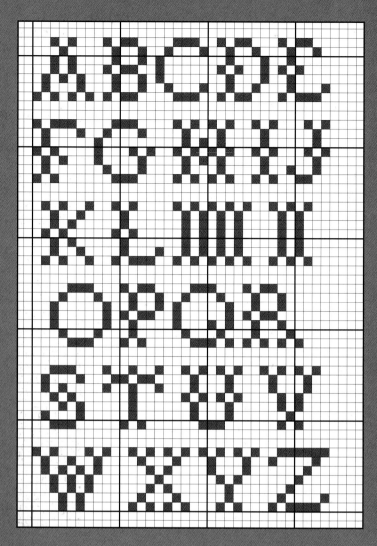

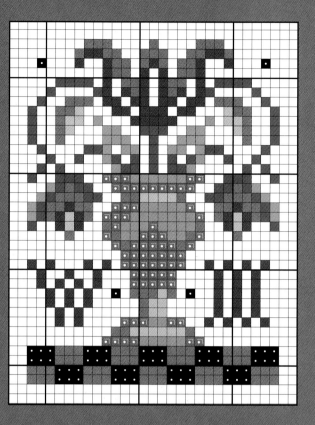

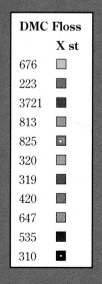

DMC Floss

X st

676	
223	
3721	
813	
825	
320	
319	
420	
647	
535	
310	

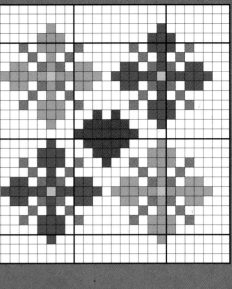

DMC Floss			
	X st	**BS**	**FK**
746	☐		
745	H		
676	▨		
353	−		
818	△		
776	▨		
899	▨		
321	◻		
498	★		
815		⌐	
223	▨		
3721		⌐	●
211	☐		
209	▨		
747	☐		
3766	◉		
807	▨		
800	+		
809	▨		
813	▨		
825	▣		
320	▨		
319	▨	⌐	
420	▨		
647	▨		
535	■	⌐	
414		⌐	
3799	✳	⌐	
310	■		●

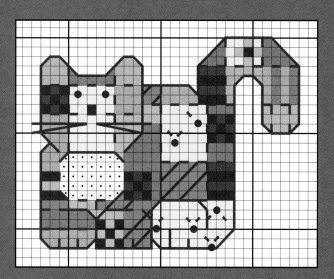

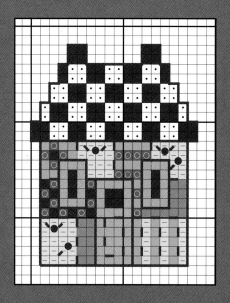

DMC Floss

	X st	FK		X st	BS	FK
White	·		797	■		
677	□		796		⌐	
676	▨		772	⊟		
3779	▨		3810	▨	⌐	
3778	▨		959	▨		
209	◉		3827	▨		
553	■	●	977	＋		
809	▨		413	■	⌐	●
798	▨		310	■	⌐	

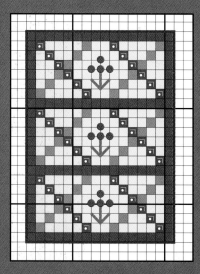

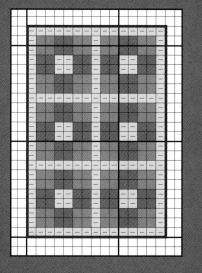

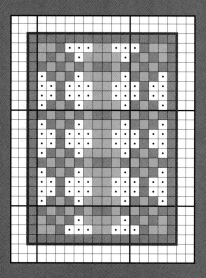

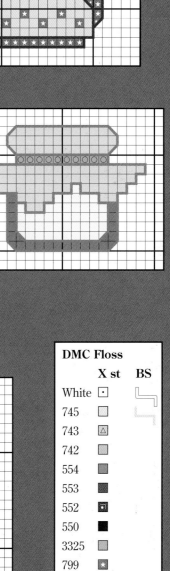

DMC Floss

	X st	BS
White	⊡	⌐
745	☐	⌐
743	△	
742	☐	
554	☐	
553	☐	
552	⊡	
550	■	
3325	☐	
799	✦	
747	☐	
3766	◎	
807	☐	⌐
3363	☐	
3053	☐	
3052	☐	
3051	☐	
563	☐	
561	☐	
400	■	
413		⌐

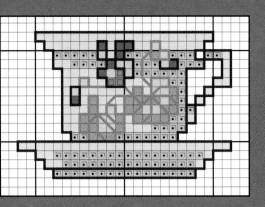

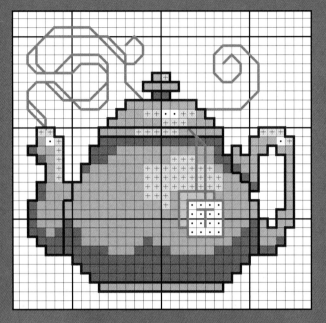

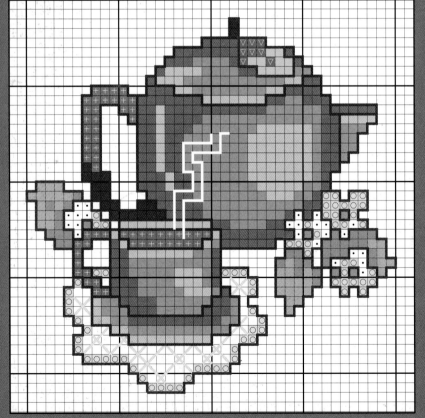

DMC Floss

	X st	BS		X st	BS
White	·	⌐	813	▨	
744	⊙		825	▨	⌐
742	▨		3364	▨	
741	▨		3363	▨	
740	▨		368	▨	
818	▨		367	▽	
776	⊡		504	▨	
3713	+		502	▨	
760	▨		501		⌐
3328	▨		3776	+	
347		⌐	400	▨	
3747	▨		918		⌐
341	▣		762	▨	
340	▨		414		⌐
333		⌐	413		⌐
827	N				

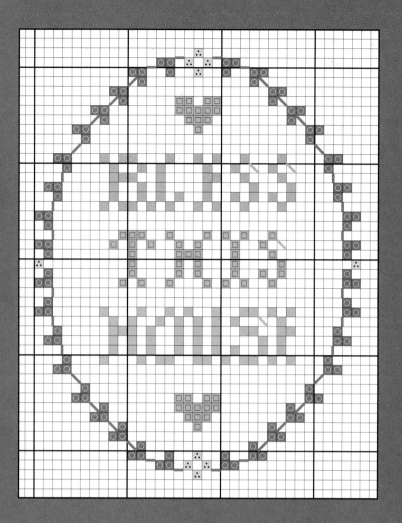

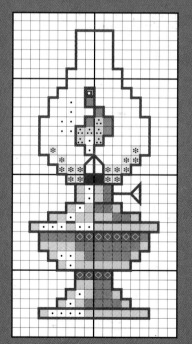

DMC Floss

	X st	BS		X st	BS
White	⊡		954	▦	
745	✳		911	�◼	
743	⊡		402	▦	⌐
970	▦		3776	⊞	
760	▣	⌐	762	▢	
3731	▦	⌐	318	▨	
606	▣	⌐	317	◇	
210	▦	⌐	413	◼	⌐
367	◉	⌐			

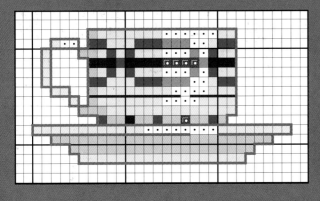

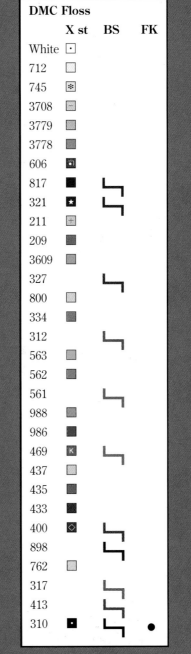

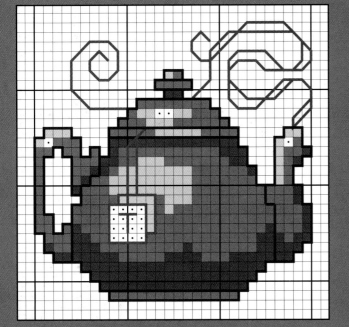

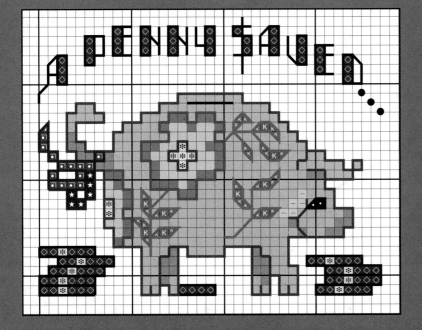

DMC Floss			
	X st	BS	FK
White	·		
712			
745	✳		
3708	–		
3779			
3778			
606	⬓		
817	■	⌐	
321	★	⌐	
211	+		
209			
3609			
327		⌐	
800			
334		⌐	
312		⌐	
563			
562			
561		⌐	
988			
986			
469	K	⌐	
437			
435			
433			
400	◇	⌐	
898		⌐	
762			
317		⌐	
413		⌐	
310	■	⌐	●

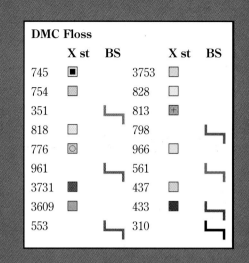

DMC Floss

	X st	BS		X st	BS
745	■		3753	▨	
754	▨		828	▢	
351		⌐	813	⊞	
818	▢		798		
776	◉		966	▨	
961		⌐	561		⌐
3731	▨		437	▨	
3609	▨		433	■	⌐
553		⌐	310		⌐

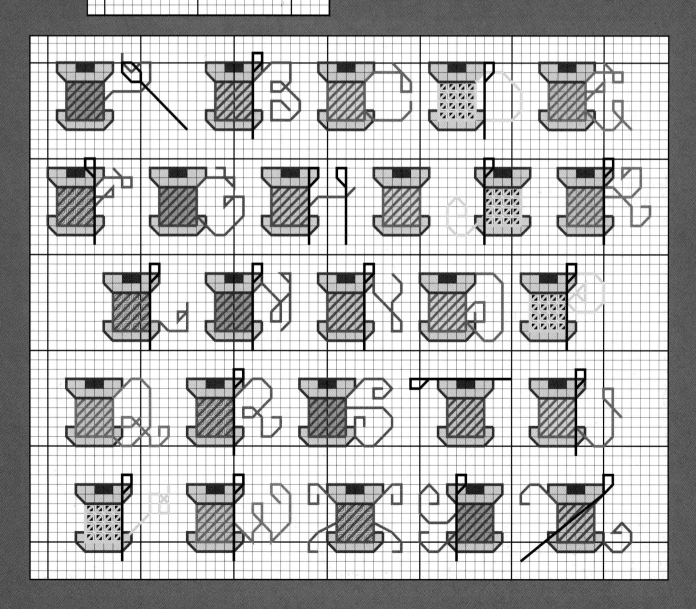

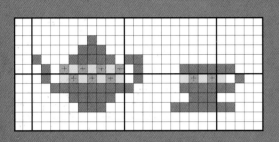

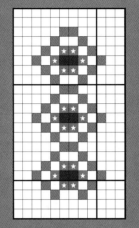

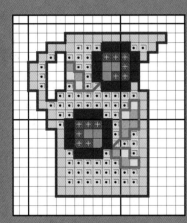

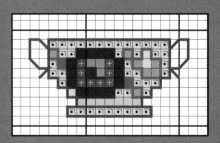

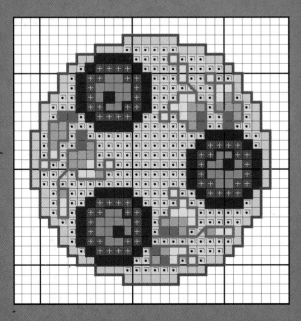

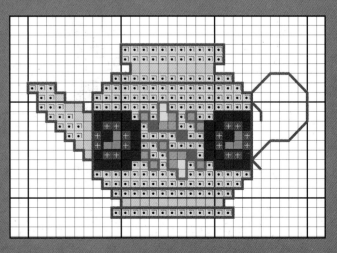

DMC Floss

	X st	BS		X st	BS
White	·		826	▨	⌐
744	△		825	▨	
743	+	⌐	798	⊡	
742	▨		564	⊠	
970	▨		563	▨	
606	+		3348	▨	
817	■	⌐	988	▨	
3609	▨		469	▨	
340	★		986	▨	⌐
333	■		739	▨	
828	▨		436	▨	
827	⊡		433	■	⌐
775	▨		414		⌐
813	▨		317		⌐

66

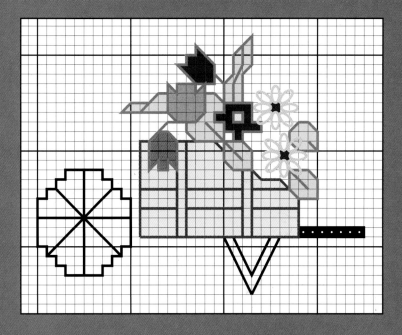

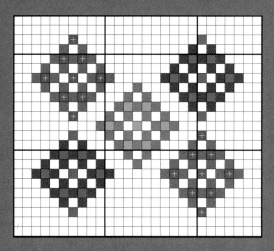

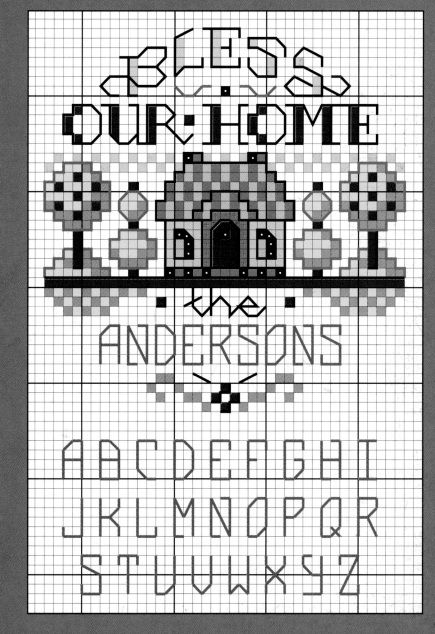

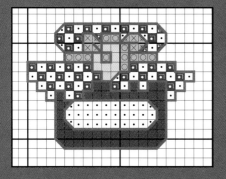
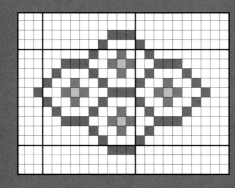
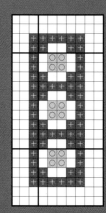

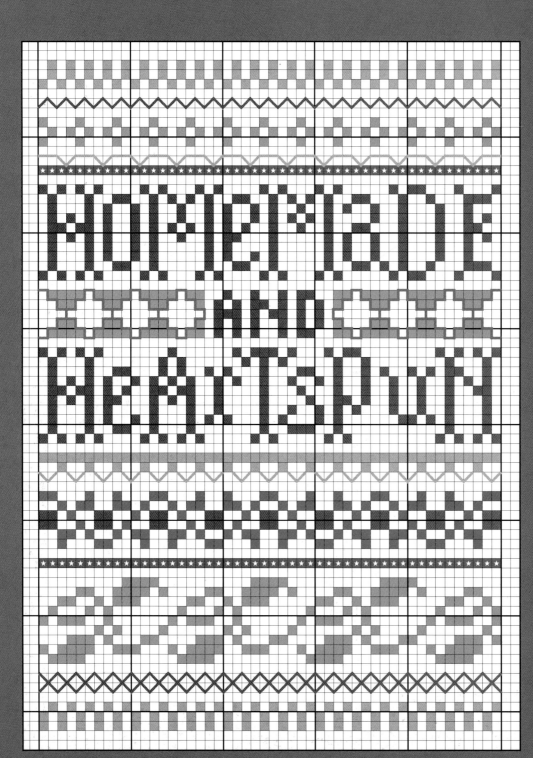

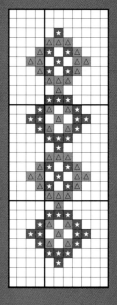

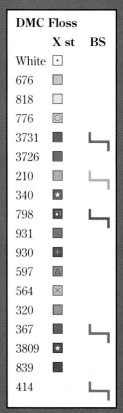

DMC Floss		
	X st	BS
White	⊡	
676		
818		
776	◎	
3731		⌐
3726		
210		⌐
340	★	
798	▣	⌐
931		
930	+	
597		
564	⊠	
320		
367		⌐
3809	★	
839		
414		⌐

DMC Floss

	X st	BS		X st	BS	FK
745	▢		436	▨		
743		⌐	433	◼	⌐	
729	▨		422	⊞		
351	▣		632	◉		
350	◼		839		⌐	
347		⌐	844	▨		
800	−		762	▢		
798		⌐	318	▨		
955	◎		413	▣	⌐	●
911		⌐	310	▨	⌐	●
738	▽					

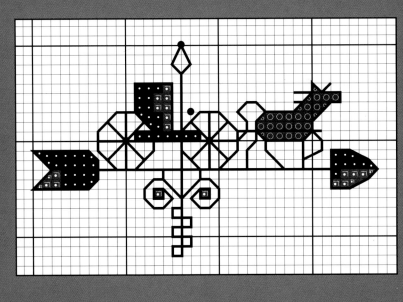

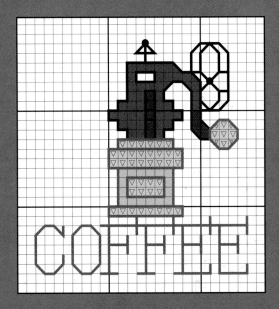

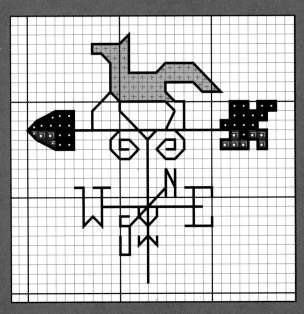

Kindred Spirits

Spirits

The World's Greatest

Bowler
Cook
Teacher
Doctor
Lawyer
Friend
Salesman
Golfer
Boss
Nurse

Always my
Daughter
now too,
my Friend

ngratulations

A Star is born

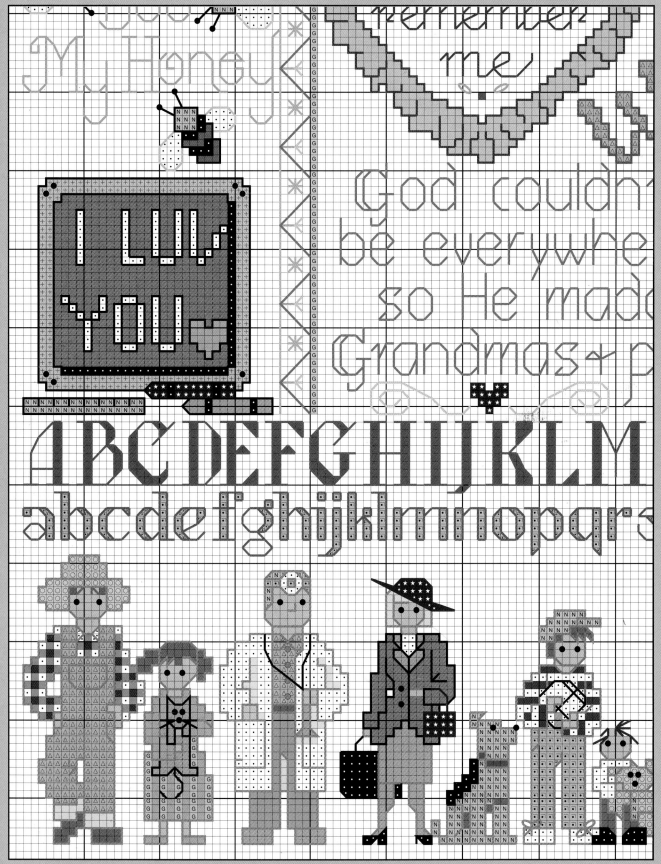

Bottom Left

Bottom Right

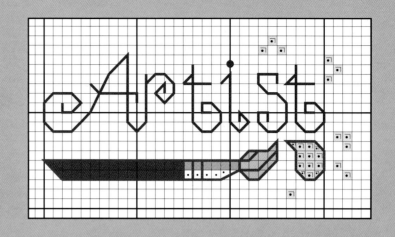

Code for Pages 72-75

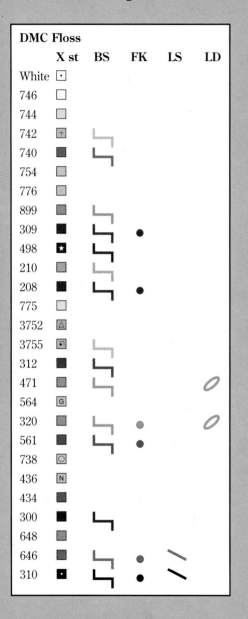

DMC Floss

	X st	BS	FK	LS	LD
White	·				
746	☐				
744	☐				
742	⊞				
740	■	⌐			
754	☐				
776	☐				
899	■	⌐			
309	■	⌐	●		
498	★	⌐			
210	■	⌐			
208	■	⌐	●		
775	☐				
3752	△				
3755	▣	⌐			
312	■	⌐			
471	■	⌐		0	
564	G				
320	■	⌐	●	0	
561	■	⌐	●		
738	○				
436	N				
434	■				
300	■	⌐			
648	■				
646	■	⌐	●	╱	
310	▪	⌐	●	╱	

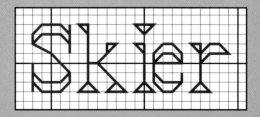

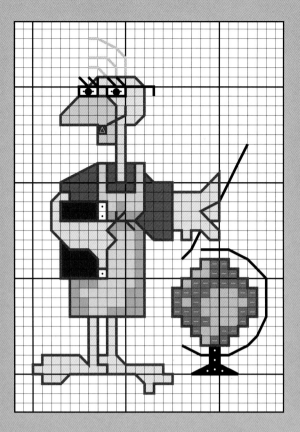

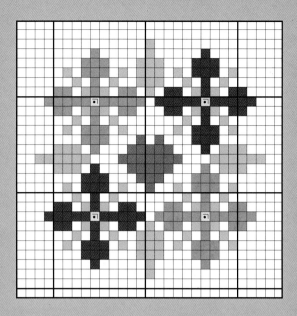

Code for Pages 76-77

DMC Floss

	X st		X st	BS	FK
White	⊡	797		⌐	●
745		747			
727	⊡	959			
725		3765			
3712	+	955	◎		
349	■	502			
3609		436			
3607		976			
931		415			
930	⊡	3799	△	⌐	
799	⊟	310	■	└	●
798					

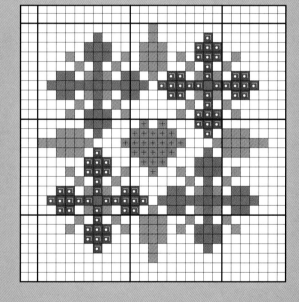

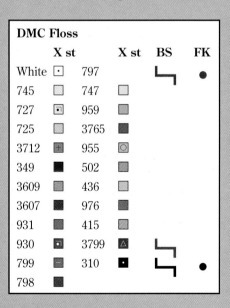

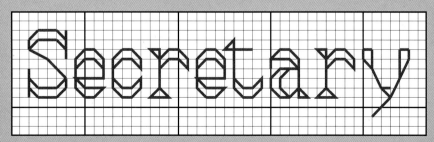

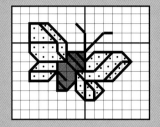

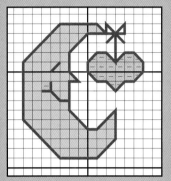

DMC Floss

	X st	BS	FK
White	⊡		
746	☐		
744		⌐	
743	☐		
951	☐		
776	⊟		
3609	▨		
350	▨		
800	☐		
334	⊡		
312		⌐	
964	☐		
958	▨		
435	▨		
839	▨		
646		⌐	●
3799		⌐	
310	■	⌐	●

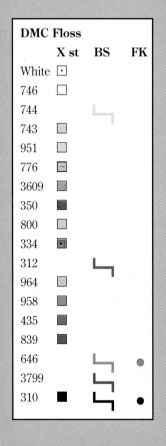

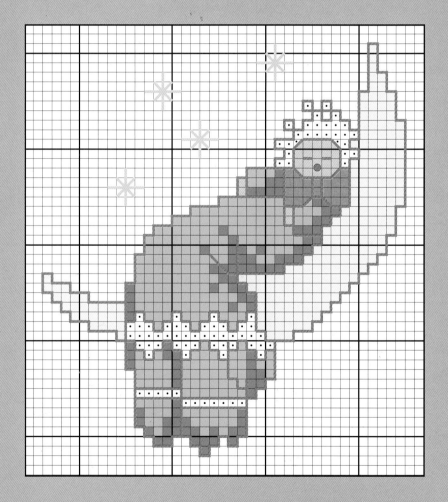

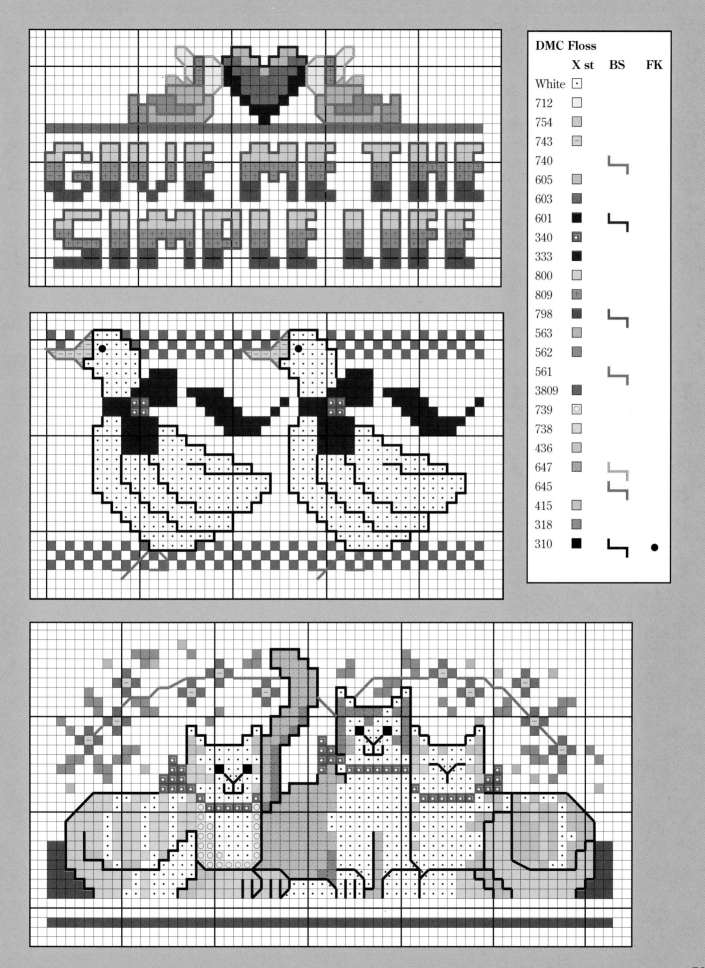

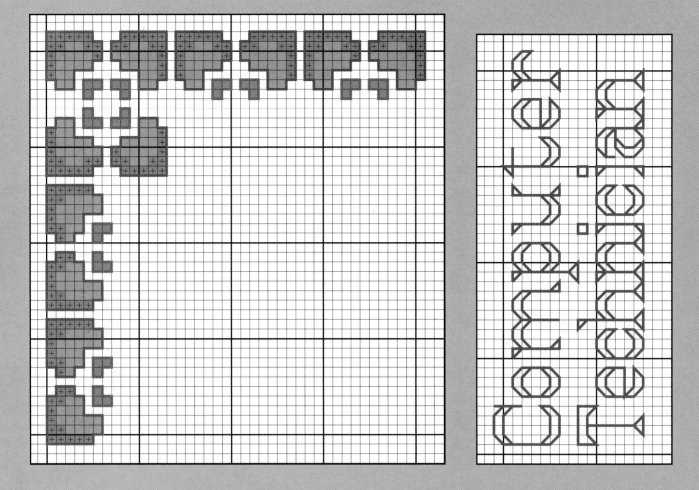

DMC Floss

	X st	BS	FK
White	·		
3823			
745			
744			
818			
3326			
899	+		
335		⌐	
211			
209			
564			
562			
989			
987		⌐	
700		⌐	
433		⌐	●
317		⌐	
3799		⌐	
310	■	⌐	●

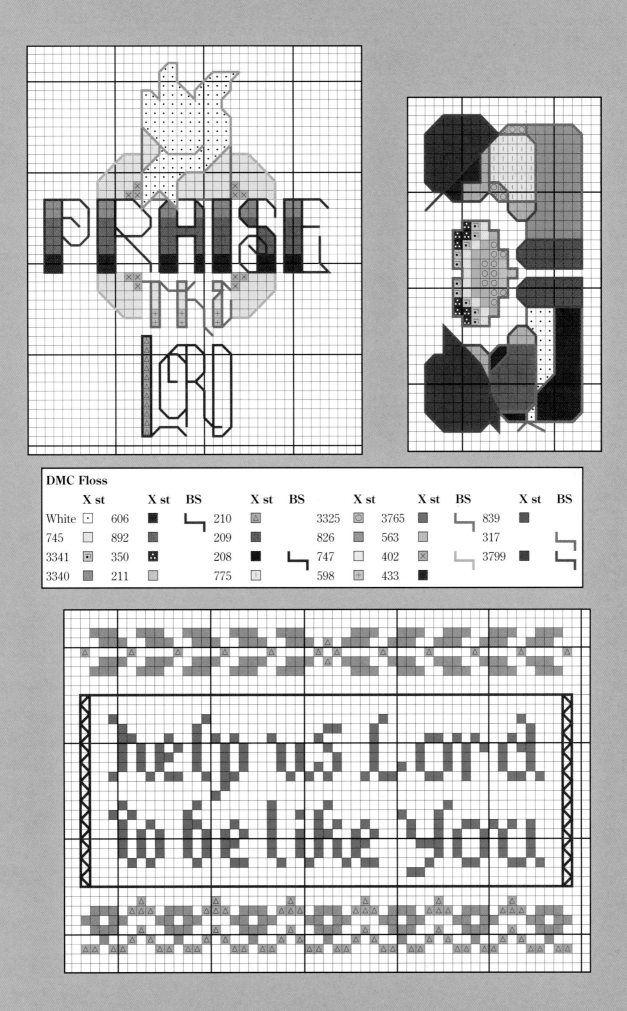

DMC Floss

X st		X st	BS	X st	BS	X st		X st	BS	X st	BS
White ⊡	606 ■	210 ⊿		3325 ⊙	3765 ■	839 ■					
745 ▨	892 ▨	209 ▨		826 ▨	563 ▨	317					
3341 ▣	350 ▧	208 ■		747 ▢	402 ⊠	3799 ■					
3340 ▨	211 ▨	775 ⌶		598 ▨	433 ⊞	■					

DMC Floss

	X st		X st		X st		X st	BS		X st		X st		X st	BS		X st	BS
White	·	3326		3766		312			738	921		841			762			
3045		666		322		989			402	842	+	938			310	·		

DMC Floss

	X st	BS		X st	BS	FK
White	·		3761	⊞		
745			797		⌐	
740		⌐	3765		⌐	
3689	◎		772	▫	⌐	
3688	▨		988		⌐	
3687		⌐	435	▨		
3607		⌐	413	■	⌐	●
349	■	⌐				

DMC Floss

	X st		X st	BS		X st	BS		X st	BS		X st	BS	FK
White	·	350	+		824			435			3799				●
745		817	■		3766			762			413				●
225		3753			436			414			310				
351		799												

84

DMC Floss

	X st	BS		X st	BS
White	·		813	▨	
744			826	N	
945			824		⌐
402	+		964	▫	
776			959	▨	
899			966		
211			563	⋰	
210	◎		319		
209			610	▨	
208		⌐	801	■	⌐
3753	⊡		413		⌐
827					

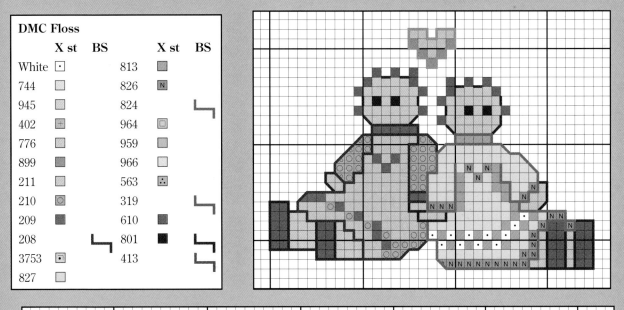

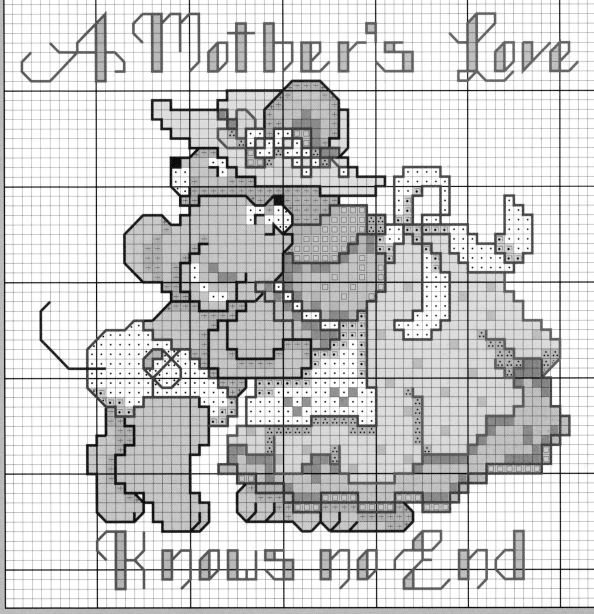

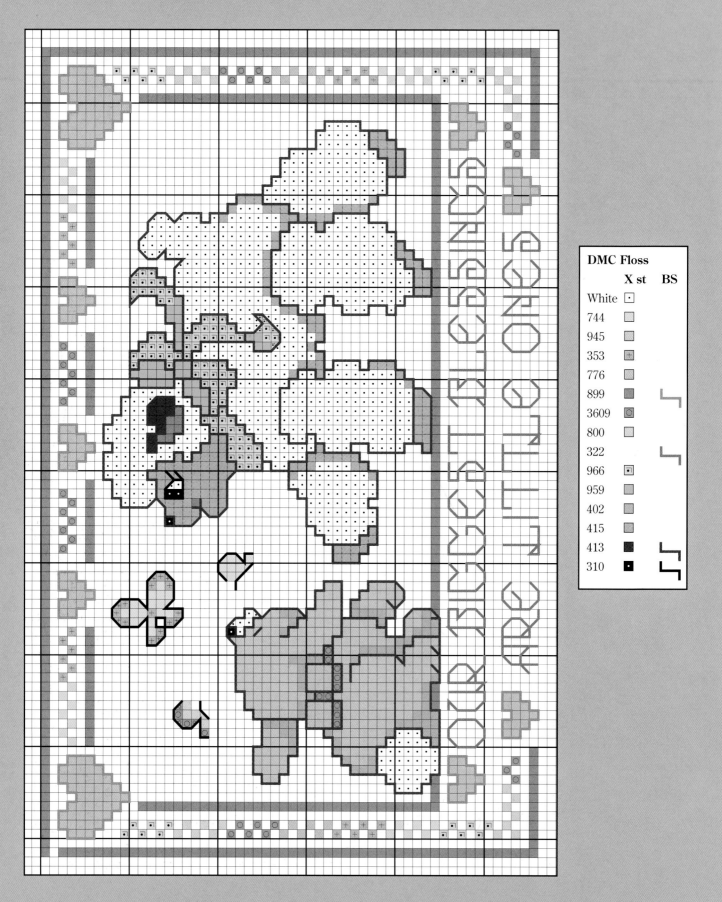

DMC Floss		
	X st	BS
White	·	
744		
945		
353	+	
776		
899		⌐
3609	⊙	
800		⌐
322		⌐
966	⊡	
959		
402		
415		
413	■	⌐
310	■	⌐

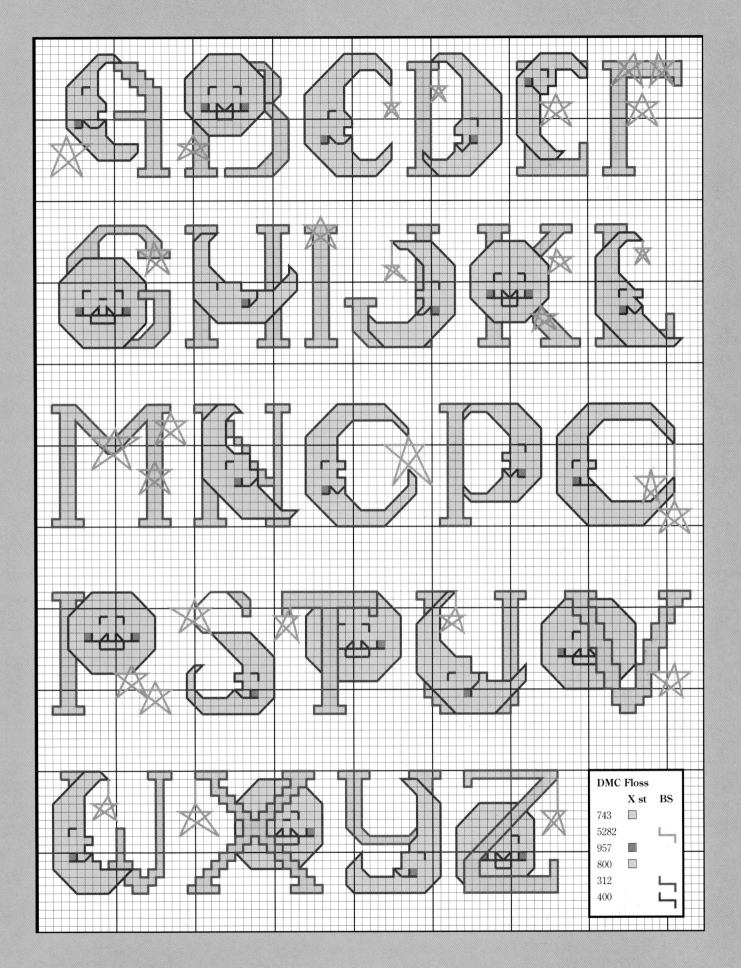

DMC Floss

	X st	BS
743		
5282		
957		
800		
312		
400		

Love & Friendship

Welcome to our WORLD

The G...

Because of you the WORLD is a little sweeter

God Bless

A FRIEND is a present you give yourself

LOVE

HOPE

CHARIT

Bottom Left

92

Bottom Right

Code for Pages 90-93

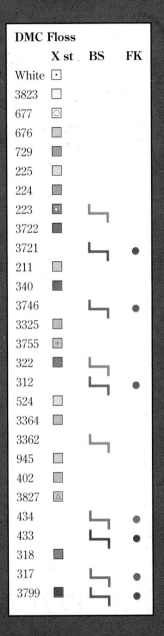

DMC Floss

	X st	BS	FK
White	⊡		
3823	☐		
677	◎		
676	▨		
729	▨		
225	▨		
224	▨		
223	⊡	⌐	
3722	▨		
3721		⌐	●
211	▨		
340	▨		
3746		⌐	●
3325	▨		
3755	⊞		
322	▨	⌐	
312	▨	⌐	●
524	▨		
3364	▨		
3362		⌐	
945	▨		
402	▨		
3827	△		
434		⌐	●
433		⌐	●
318	▨	⌐	
317		⌐	●
3799	■	⌐	●

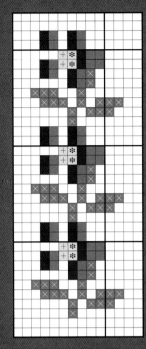

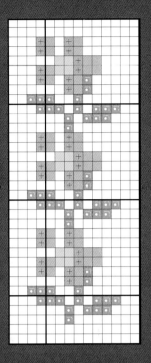

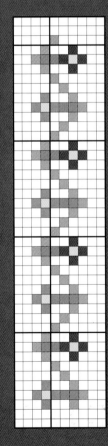

Code for Pages 94-95

DMC Floss

	X st	BS
745	▨	
744	▨	
743	◎	
742	▨	
727	❊	
726	⊞	
761	▨	
760	⊞	
3350	■	
554	▨	
552	■	
340	▨	
333	■	
320	⊡	
502	▨	
501	▨	
911	⊠	
434		⌐

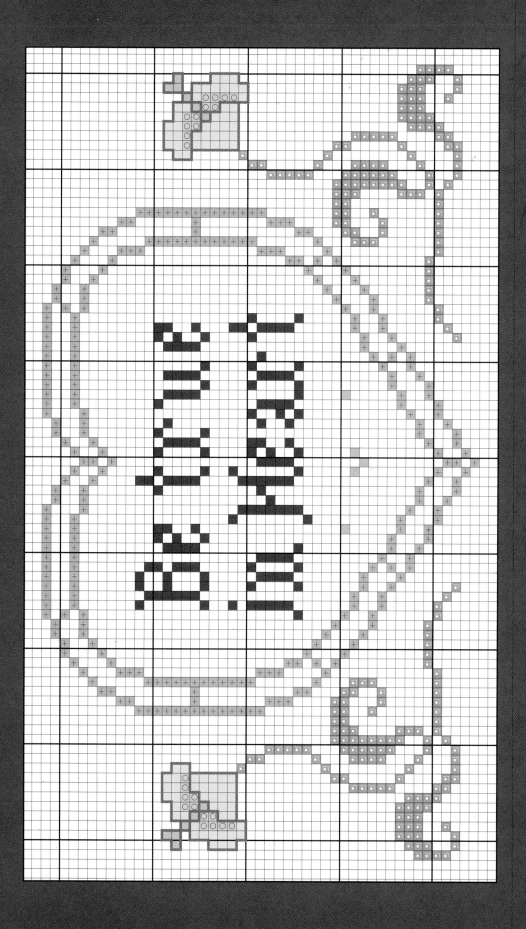

Code for Page 96

DMC Floss

	X st	BS	Bds
White	⊡		
745	▫		
743	▣		
676	⊞		
948	▫		
754	▪		
758	⊟		
3326	▪		
3607	■		
3756	▫		
800	▪		
3755	⊡		
322	▪		
312	■	⌐	
3347	▪		
3346	◉		
3345		⌐⌐	
301		⌐⌐	
317		⌐⌐	
White			⊠
Silver			▪

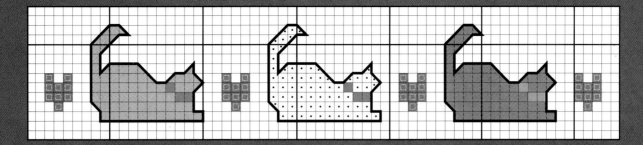

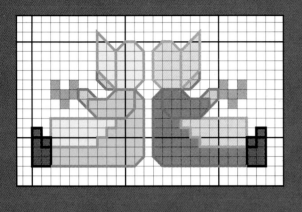

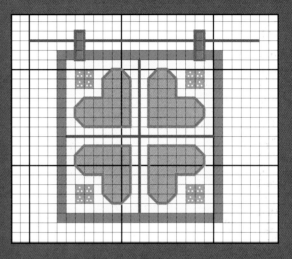

DMC Floss

	X st	BS	FK
White	⊡		
3823	☐		
745	⊟		
743	▦		
741	▩	⌐	
754	▨		
225	▤		
224	▦	⌐	
223	▦		
3722	▣	⌐	
3761	☐		
519	▢		
518	▨	⌐	
3760	▦	⌐	
517	■	⌐	●
3816	▨		
3815	▦		
500		⌐	
435	▨		
839	▦		
310		⌐	●

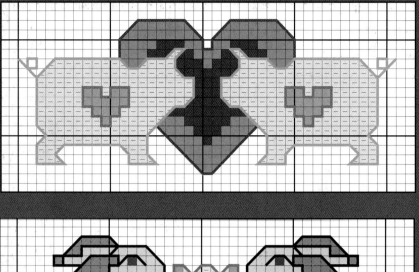

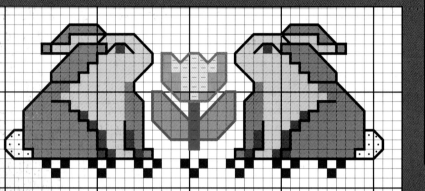

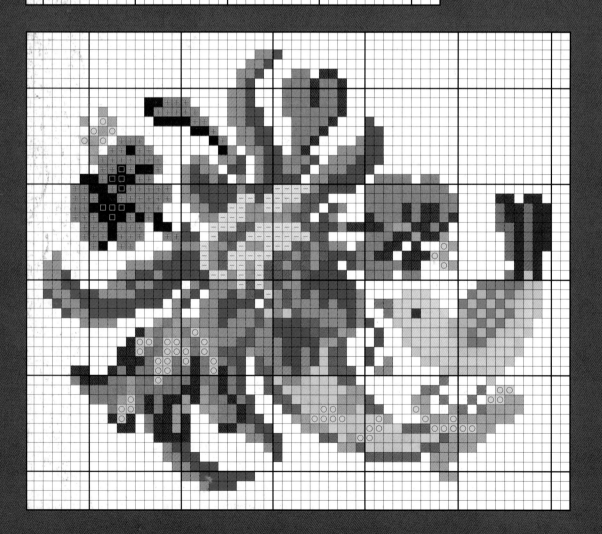

DMC Floss					
	X st	BS		X st	BS
White	·		825	■	
743	◎		993	■	
818	−		3814	■	
3354	■	⌐	988	■	
3722	■	⌐	986	■	⌐
3712	✝		3773	■	
347	■		738	■	
816	◻		436	■	
554	■		762	■	
552	■	⌐	318	■	
3753	■		413	■	
827	■		310		⌐

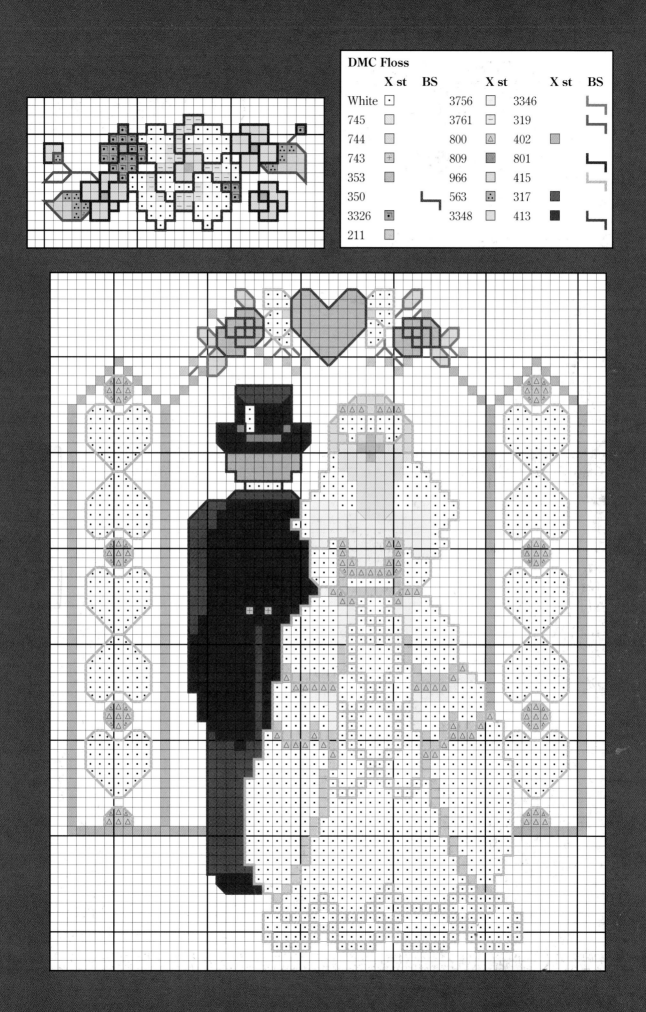

DMC Floss

	X st	BS		X st	BS	FK
White	·		208	■	⌐	
745	−		563	▨		
744	△		562	❋		
819	◿		561	E		
818	▫		772	▫		
776	+		989	▨		
963	⊠		987	▨		
962	⊡		986	■	⌐	
961		⌐	739	▫		
335		⌐	435	▨		
352	▨		839	■		
351	❋		3773	▨		
498	❤	⌐	3772	▨		
349	■		898	⊡	⌐	
210	⊙		317		⌐	
209	▨		310		⌐	●

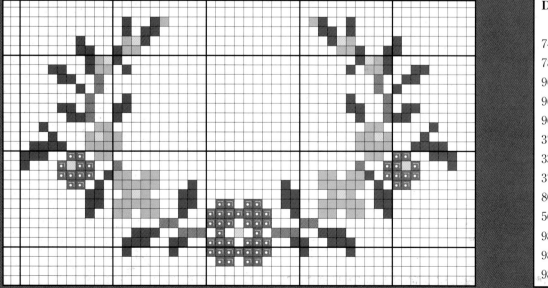

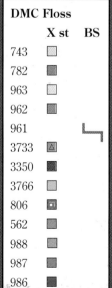

DMC Floss

	X st	BS
743	▢	
782	▨	
963	▢	
962	▨	
961		⌐
3733	△	
3350	▨	
3766	▢	
806	▣	
562	▨	
988	▨	
987	▨	
986	▨	

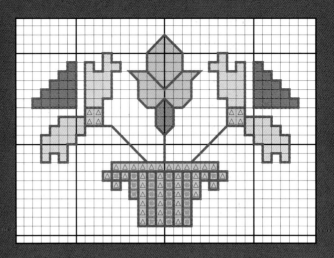

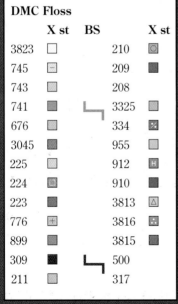

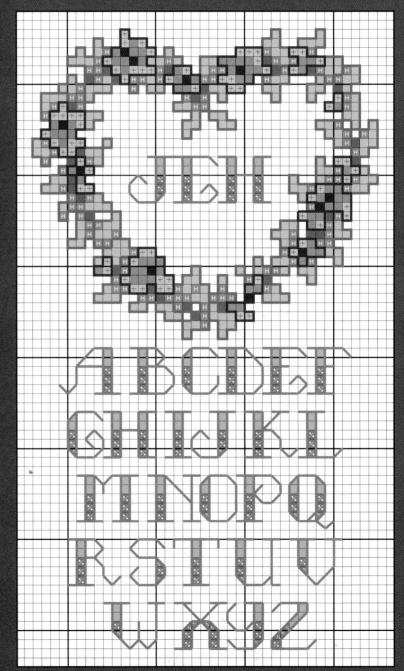

DMC Floss

	X st	BS		X st
3823	☐		210	◉
745	−		209	■
743	▨		208	
741	■	⌐	3325	▨
676	▨		334	▨
3045	■		955	▨
225	▨		912	H
224	▣		910	■
223	■		3813	△
776	+		3816	▨
899	■		3815	■
309	■	⌐	500	
211	▨		317	

102

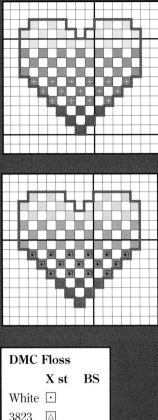

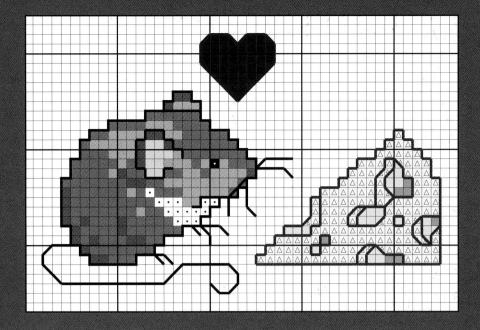

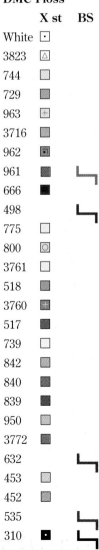

DMC Floss

	X st	BS
White	⊡	
3823	△	
744	▢	
729	▨	
963	+	
3716	▨	
962	⊡	
961	◪	
666	◼	⌐
498		⌐
775	▢	
800	◎	
3761	▢	
518	▨	
3760	+	
517	◪	
739	▢	
842	▨	
840	▨	
839	◪	
950	▨	
3772	▨	
632		⌐
453	▢	
452	▨	
535		⌐
310	◼	⌐

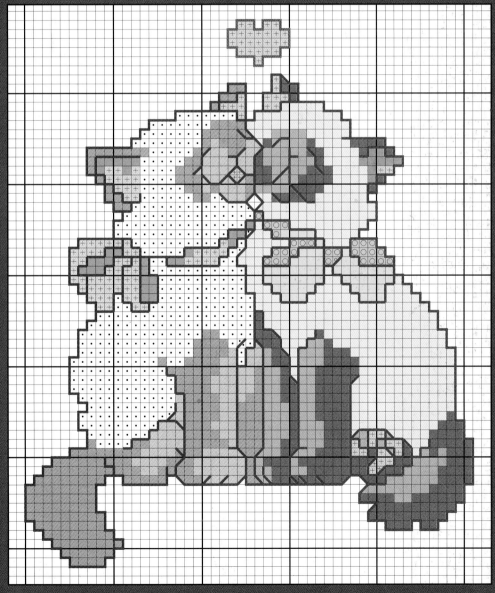

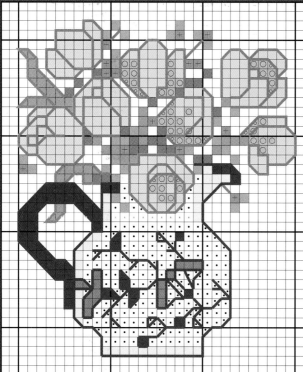

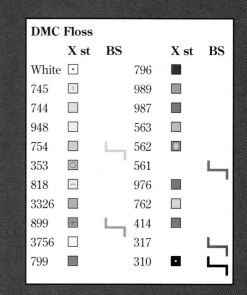

DMC Floss

	X st	BS		X st	BS
White	·		796	■	
745			989		
744			987		
948			563		
754		⌐	562		
353	◎		561		⌐
818	−		976		
3326			762		
899	+	⌐	414		
3756			317		⌐
799			310	■	⌐

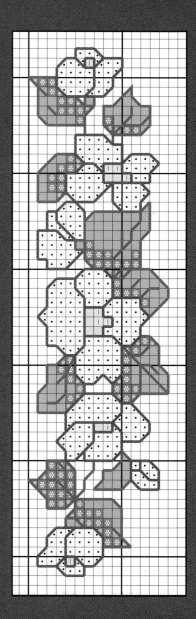

DMC Floss

	X st	BS	FK
White	⊡		
3823	☐		
744	▨		
722	▨	⌐	
720	▨		
818	⊟		
776	▨		
3326	▣		
309		⌐	
3688	▨		
3803	▨		
931	▨		
3064	▨		
632	■		
801	◉		
3024	▨		
648	▨		
647	▦		
415	⊡		
451	▨		
535	■		
310	■	⌐	●

105

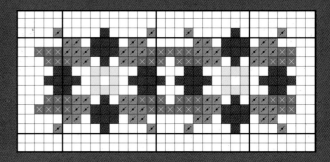

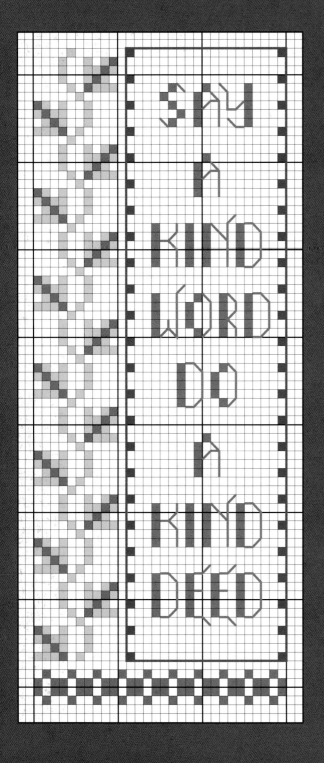

SAY A KIND LORD DO A KIND DEED

DMC Floss				
	X st	**BS**	**X st**	**BS**
White	·	792	■	⌐
3823	□	368	▨	
745	✳	367	▨	
727	▨	911	✕	
3045	⌐	3364	▨	
818	−	3363	⊡	
3326	▨	3779	−	
3733	◪	3778	⊙	
3350	■	317	⌐	
211	▨	413	⌐	
209	▨	⌐		

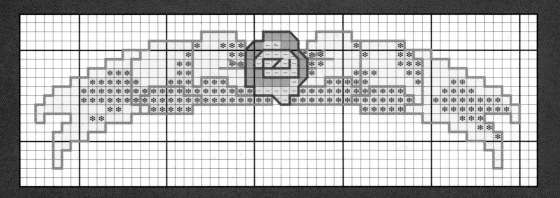

DMC Floss

	X st		X st	BS
White	·	825		
743		809		
349		469		
827				

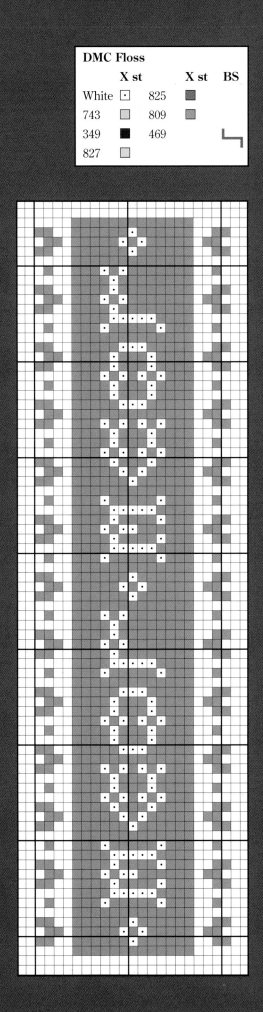

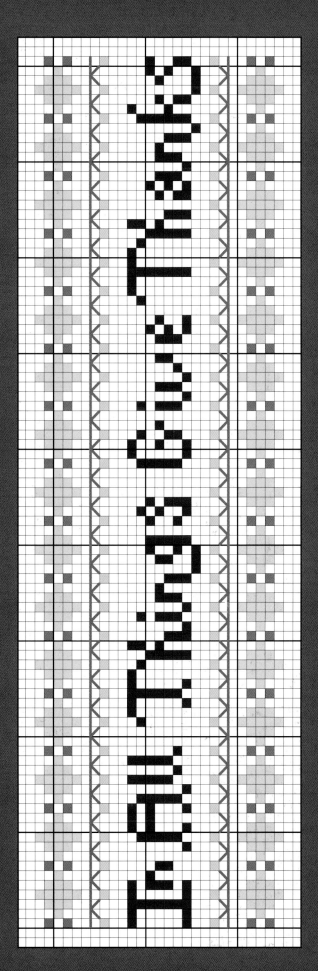

Mother Nature

Make our Earth
an Eden
like the heavens
above

Bottom Left

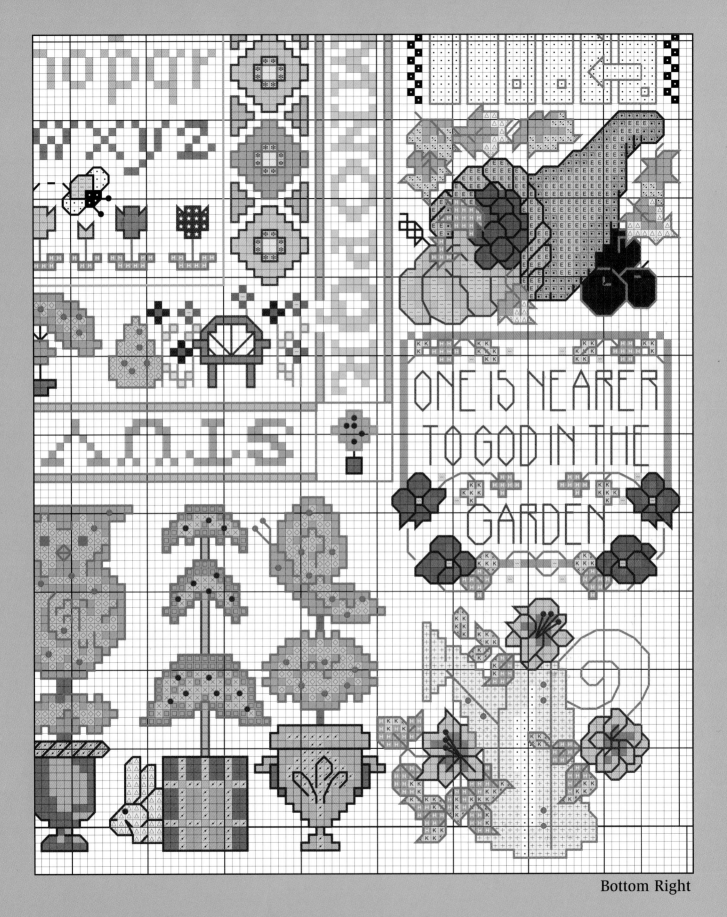

ONE IS NEARER TO GOD IN THE GARDEN

Bottom Right

Code for Pages 110-113

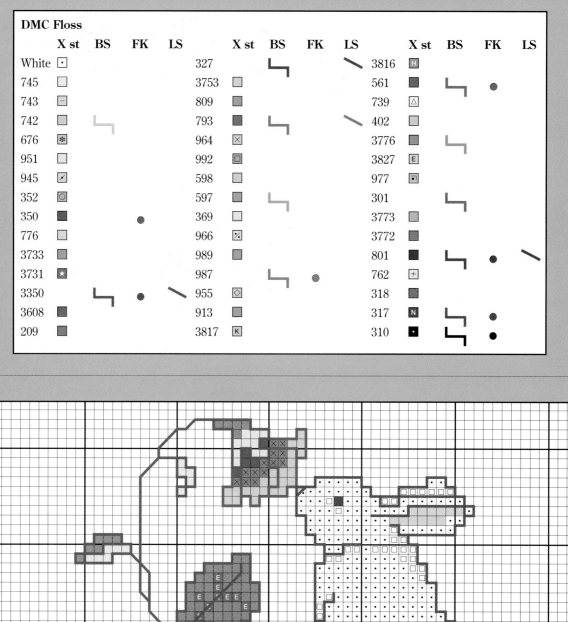

DMC Floss

	X st	BS	FK	LS		X st	BS	FK	LS		X st	BS	FK	LS
White	·				327		⌐		╲	3816	⊞			
745	▫				3753	▫				561	▪	⌐	●	
743	⊟				809	▪				739	△			
742	▫	⌐			793	▪	⌐			402	▫			╲
676	✳				964	⊠				3776	▪	⌐		
951	▫				992	⊡				3827	E			
945	◢				598	▫				977	⊡			
352	⊙				597	▪	⌐			301		⌐		
350	▨		●		369	▫				3773	▫			
776	▫				966	▨				3772	▪			
3733	▪				989	▪	⌐			801	▪	⌐	●	╲
3731	★				987		⌐	●		762	⊞			
3350		⌐	●	╲	955	◇				318	▨			
3608	▨				913	▪				317	N	⌐	●	
209	▪				3817	K				310	■	⌐	●	

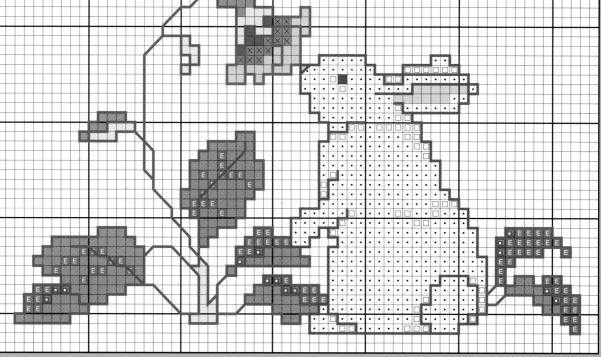

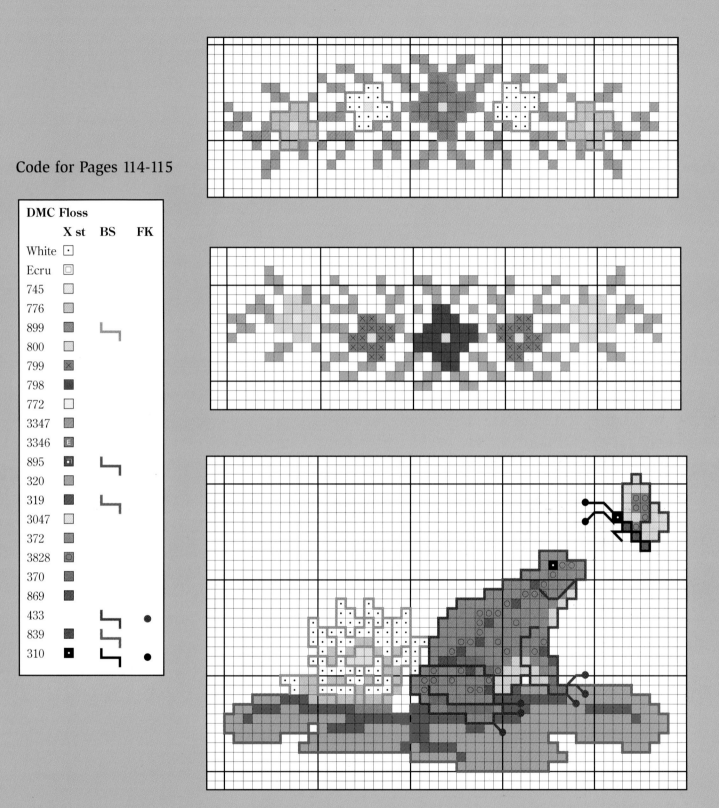

Code for Pages 114-115

DMC Floss

	X st	BS	FK
White	⊡		
Ecru	▣		
745	▨		
776	▨		
899	▨	⌐	
800	▨		
799	⊠		
798	▩		
772	☐		
3347	▨		
3346	▣		
895	▣	⌐	
320	▨		
319	▩	⌐	
3047	▨		
372	▨		
3828	◉		
370	▨		
869	▩		
433	▨	⌐	●
839	▩	⌐	
310	▣	⌐	●

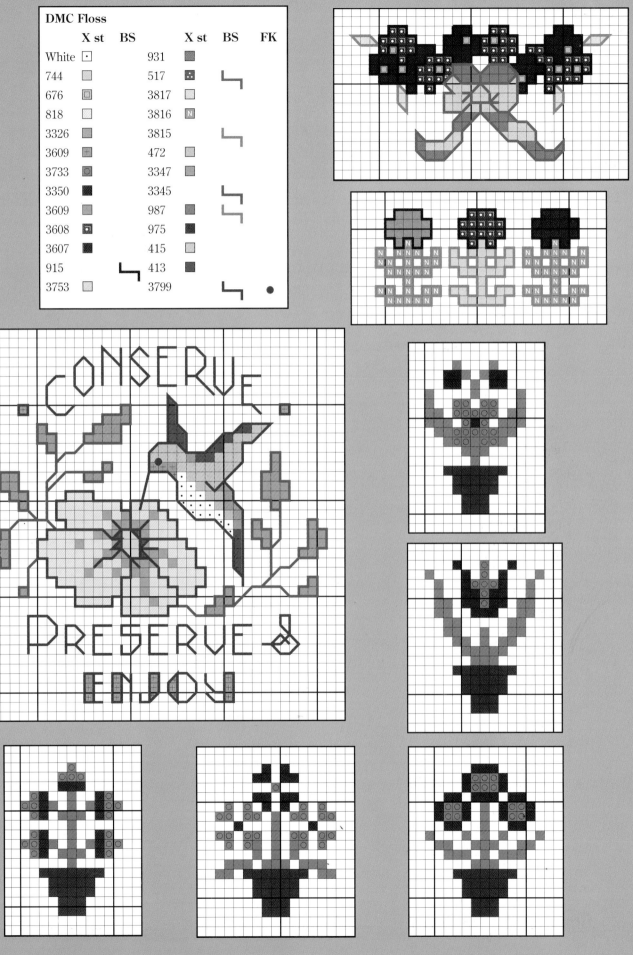

DMC Floss

	X st	BS		X st	BS	FK
White	·		931			
744			517		⌐	
676			3817			
818			3816	N		
3326			3815		⌐	
3609	+		472			
3733	◎		3347			
3350			3345		⌐	
3609			987			
3608	⊡		975			
3607			415			
915		⌐	413			
3753			3799		⌐	●

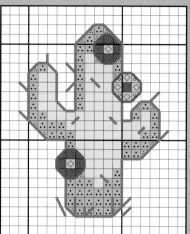

DMC Floss

	X st	BS		X st	BS		X st	BS
725	◇		930	■	⌐	3348	□	
783	■		799	▽		987	□	⌐
3609	■		797	■	⌐	368	□	
351	■	⌐	747	□		367	■	
224	▨		959	⊡		402	■	
223	■		597	■		3776	■	
221	■	⌐	806	■	⌐	301	■	
3753	▨		3810	■		801	■	⌐
932	■		772	□		414	■	⌐
931	⊞							

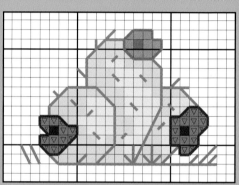

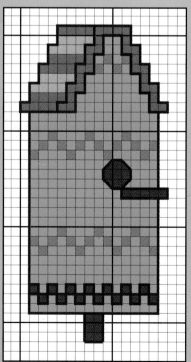

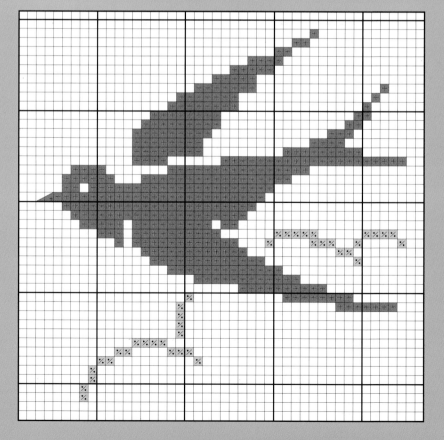

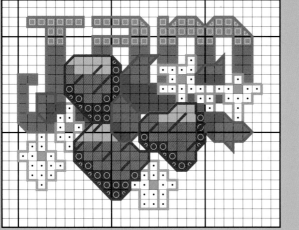

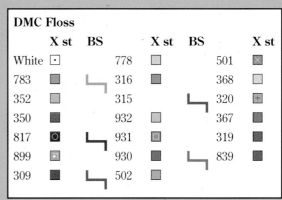

DMC Floss

	X st	BS		X st	BS		X st
White	·		778			501	
783			316			368	
352		⌐	315			320	⌐
350			932			367	
817	⊙		931		⌐	319	
899		⌐	930			839	
309		⌐	502				

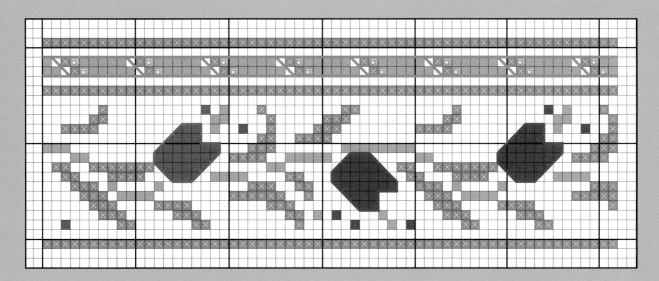

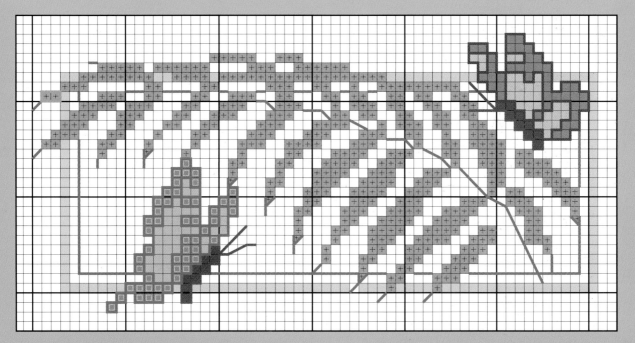

DMC Floss

	X st	BS		X st	BS		X st	BS
White	·		340	⊙		368		
744			333	■		367		
783		⌐	932			319		⌐
761			931	◉		613		⌐
760	=		503			612		
3328		⌐	502	⊞		610		⌐
817	■	⌐	501			839		⌐
341								

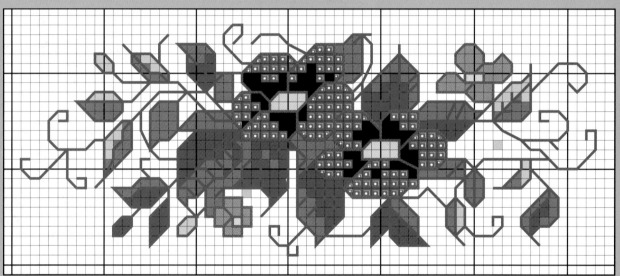

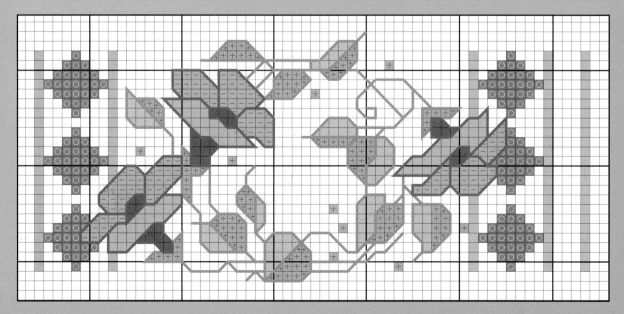

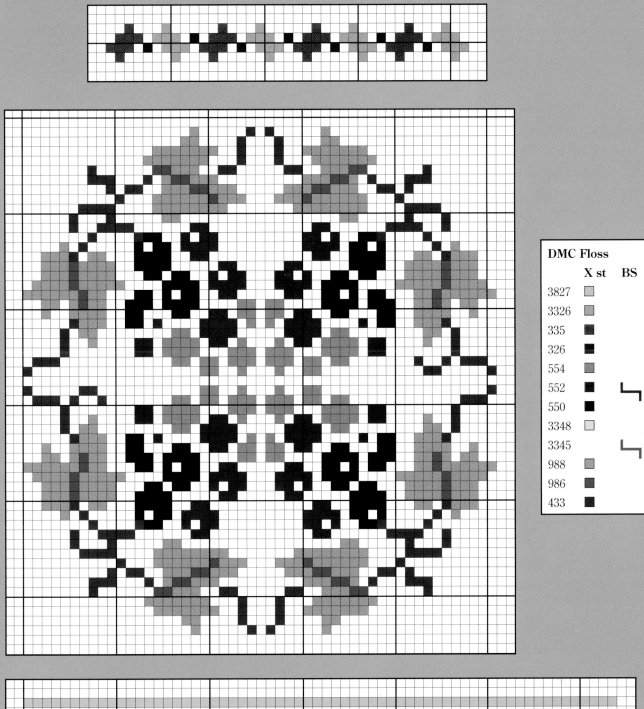

DMC Floss		
	X st	BS
3827		
3326		
335		
326		
554		
552		⌐
550		
3348		
3345		⌐
988		
986		
433		

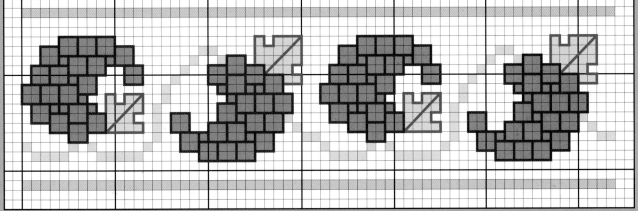

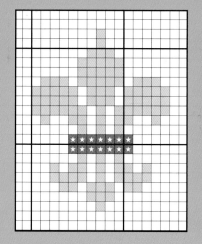

DMC Floss

	X st		X st		X st
743		760	+	550	■
783		335		988	
782	★	326	■	986	
780		554		433	
761		552			

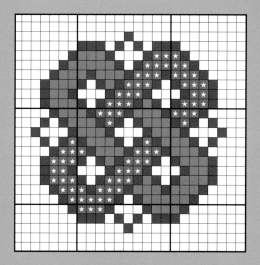

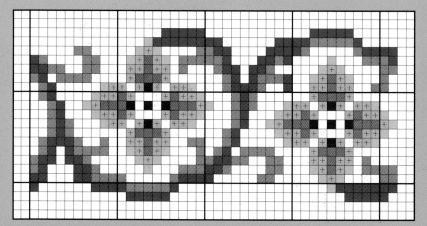

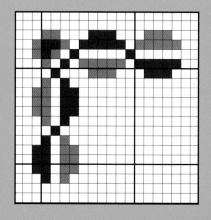

DMC Floss

	X st		X st		X st	BS	FK
White	⊡	210		825			
743		208		798	+		
741		550		975			
783	◎	3685		938	✳		●
722		3761		3799			
349		813	★	310	▪		●
900							

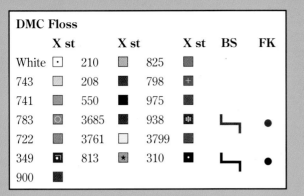

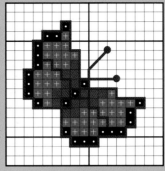

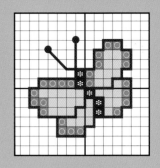

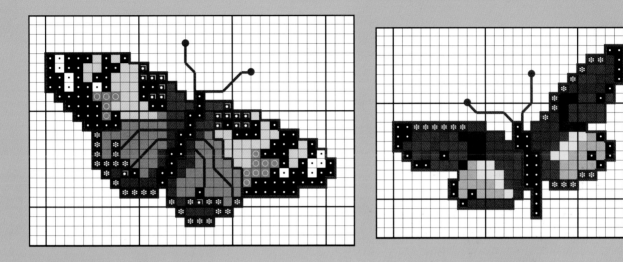

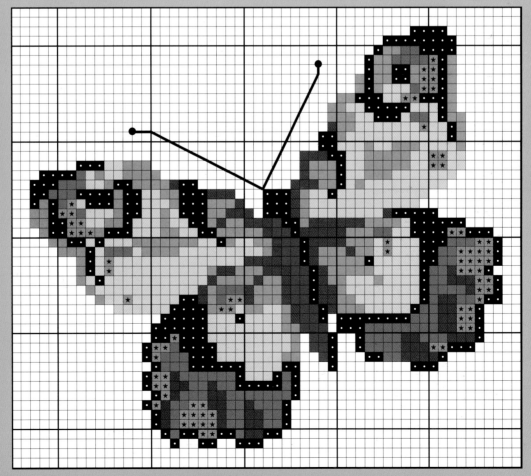

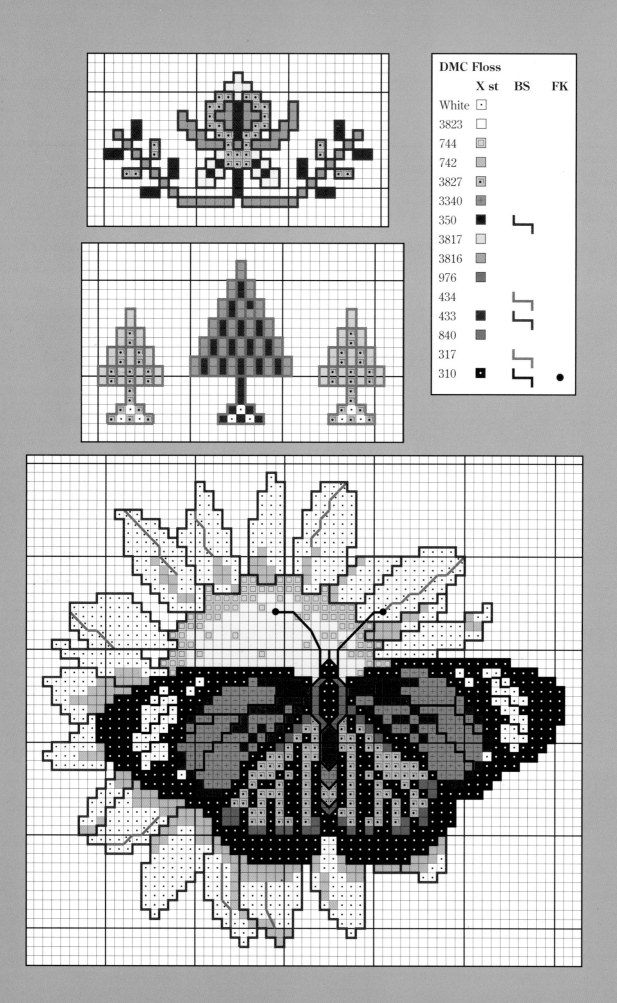

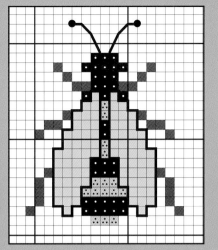

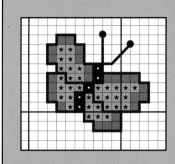

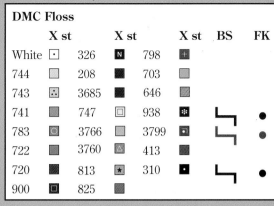

DMC Floss					
	X st		**X st**		**X st**	**BS**	**FK**
White ⊡		326 N		798 ⊞		
744		208		703		
743		3685		646		
741		747 ▢		938 ✳		
783 ◉		3766		3799 ◩		
722		3760 △		413		
720		813 ★		310 ■		
900 ▣		825				

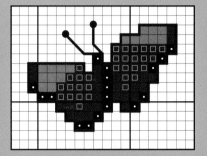

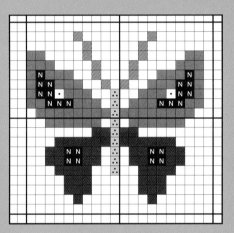

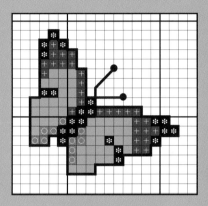

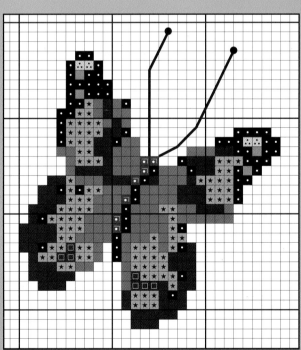

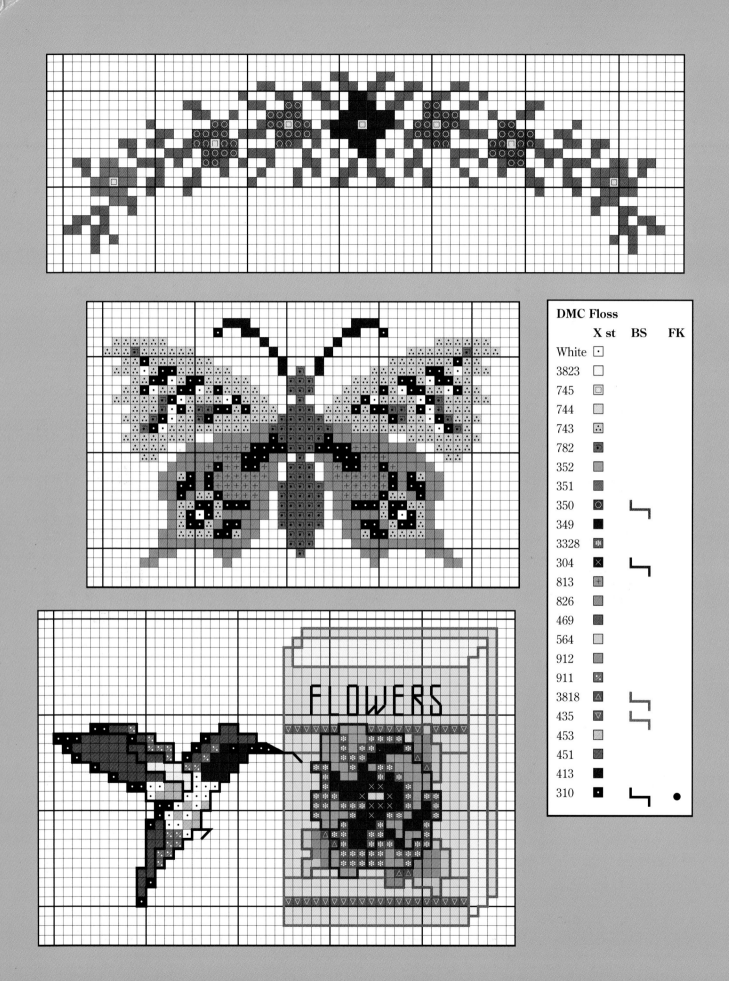

DMC Floss

	X st	BS	FK
White	⊡		
3823	□		
745	⊡		
744	▨		
743	⊡		
782	⊙		
352	▨		
351	▨		
350	⊙	⌐	
349	■		
3328	✳		
304	✕	⌐	
813	✛		
826	▨		
469	▨		
564	□		
912	▨		
911	▨		
3818	△	⌐	
435	▽	⌐	
453	□		
451	▨		
413	■		
310	■	⌐	●

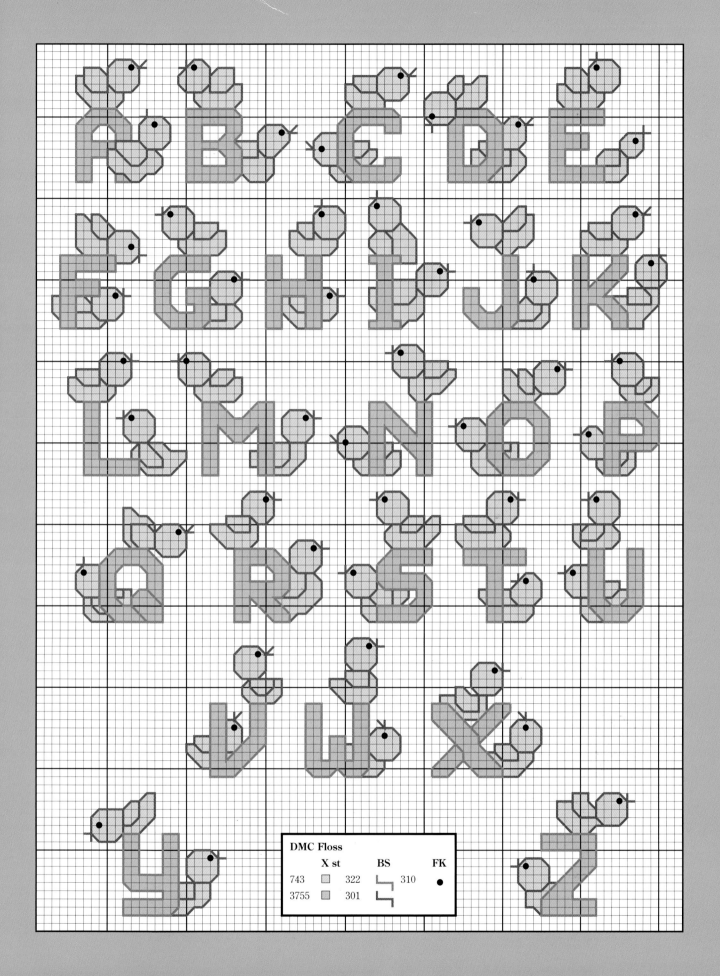

DMC Floss

	X st	BS	FK
743	☐	⌐ 310	●
3755	☐ 322	⌐	
	301		

Metric Equivalency Chart

mm-millimetres cm-centimetres
inches to millimetres and centimetres

inches	mm	cm	inches	cm	inches	cm
1/8	3	0.3	9	22.9	30	76.2
1/4	6	0.6	10	25.4	31	78.7
1/2	13	1.3	12	30.5	33	83.8
5/8	16	1.6	13	33.0	34	86.4
3/4	19	1.9	14	35.6	35	88.9
7/8	22	2.2	15	38.1	36	91.4
1	25	2.5	16	40.6	37	94.0
1 1/4	32	3.2	17	43.2	38	96.5
1 1/2	38	3.8	18	45.7	39	99.1
1 3/4	44	4.4	19	48.3	40	101.6
2	51	5.1	20	50.8	41	104.1
2 1/2	64	6.4	21	53.3	42	106.7
3	76	7.6	22	55.9	43	109.2
3 1/2	89	8.9	23	58.4	44	111.8
4	102	10.2	24	61.0	45	114.3
4 1/2	114	11.4	25	63.5	46	116.8
5	127	12.7	26	66.0	47	119.4
6	152	15.2	27	68.6	48	121.9
7	178	17.8	28	71.1	49	124.5
8	203	20.3	29	73.7	50	127.0

yards to metres

yards	metres	yards	metres	yards	metres	yards	metres	yards	metres
1/8	0.11	2 1/8	1.94	4 1/8	3.77	6 1/8	5.60	8 1/8	7.43
1/4	0.23	2 1/4	2.06	4 1/4	3.89	6 1/4	5.72	8 1/4	7.54
3/8	0.34	2 3/8	2.17	4 3/8	4.00	6 3/8	5.83	8 3/8	7.66
1/2	0.46	2 1/2	2.29	4 1/2	4.11	6 1/2	5.94	8 1/2	7.77
5/8	0.57	2 5/8	2.40	4 5/8	4.23	6 5/8	6.06	8 5/8	7.89
3/4	0.69	2 3/4	2.51	4 3/4	4.34	6 3/4	6.17	8 3/4	8.00
7/8	0.80	2 7/8	2.63	4 7/8	4.46	6 7/8	6.29	8 7/8	8.12
1	0.91	3	2.74	5	4.57	7	6.40	9	8.23
1 1/8	1.03	3 1/8	2.86	5 1/8	4.69	7 1/8	6.52	9 1/8	8.34
1 1/4	1.14	3 1/4	2.97	5 1/4	4.80	7 1/4	6.63	9 1/4	8.46
1 3/8	1.26	3 3/8	3.09	5 3/8	4.91	7 3/8	6.74	9 3/8	8.57
1 1/2	1.37	3 1/2	3.20	5 1/2	5.03	7 1/2	6.86	9 1/2	8.69
1 5/8	1.49	3 5/8	3.31	5 5/8	5.14	7 5/8	6.97	9 5/8	8.80
1 3/4	1.60	3 3/4	3.43	5 3/4	5.26	7 3/4	7.09	9 3/4	8.92
1 7/8	1.71	3 7/8	3.54	5 7/8	5.37	7 7/8	7.20	9 7/8	9.03
2	1.83	4	3.66	6	5.49	8	7.32	10	9.14

Index